The Mays | XXVII

GUEST EDITED BY
Louis de Bernières
Mary Jean Chan

STUDENT EDITORIAL TEAM
Elizabeth Huang
Eimear Ní Chathail
Caithlin Ng
Leah Wild

VARSITY PUBLICATIONS LTD

Varsity Publications Ltd
16 Mill Lane
Cambridge CB2 1RX
United Kingdom

First published 2019 by Varsity Publications Ltd
Copyright © 2019 Varsity Publications Ltd

The right of all persons so listed to be identified as the
authors of their work has been asserted by them in
accordance with the Copyright, Designs
and Patents Act of 1988

ISBN 978-0-902240-50-6

Designed and typeset
in Franziska
by Anna Dobrowolski and Dorothy Zhang

Printed and bound
by Biddles

Cover art Anna Dobrowolski

Jesus College Illustration Matthew Seccombe

British Library Cataloguing in Publication Data
A CIP catalogue record of this book
is available from the British Library.

Further copies of this book and other titles in the series
can be bought through most booksellers or direct from
Varsity Publications Ltd at the address above or at:
www.varsity.co.uk/mays
www.themaysanthology.co.uk

Contents

Editorial Team

Elizabeth Huang and Eimear Ní Chathail

DEPUTY EDITOR
Caithlin Ng

ART EDITOR
Leah Wild

SUBMISSIONS OFFICER
Lili Bidwell

POETRY SUBCOMMITTEE
Tom Bailey, Georgie Kemsley-Pein, Ben Wu, Chloe Youle

PROSE SUBCOMMITTEE
Cathy Fisher, Lilly Posnett, Rosa Rahimi, Rebecca Rochester

ART SUBCOMMITTEE
Julia Davies, Millie Horton-Insch, Emil Sands

OXFORD LIASON OFFICER
Ali Arsalan Pasha

DESIGNERS
Anna Dobrowolski and Dorothy Zhang

Foreword

It has been a great treat to read through this year's *Mays*. I was struck by the variety of the entries, some of which even provoked a pang of envy in me, alongside the admiration. 'After' is a particularly powerful piece of writing, not only because of its subject matter, but because of its presentation in parallel columns. This is the sort of experiment that people were trying out in the sixties, and have forgotten about since. Most experiments were pretentious, or didn't work, but this one does, brilliantly.

'Face, Divine' is another piece of experimentation whose wackiness belies something serious that I am still trying to tease out. The now old-fashioned use of stream of consciousness for 'birthday' perfectly portrays the strange state of mind of a schoolchild waiting for their birthday to unfold.

'I Climbed The Castle Mound' brought back memories of the anomie and stress of being a student. I clearly remember such things as the experimental consumption of three spoonfuls of instant coffee granules; that's just the sort of thing that I used to do. I remember once walking from Salford to Manchester in winter, drunk in the early hours, because there was no alternative when my girlfriend started snogging someone else at a party. We were on a terrible cheap wine called 'pornoplonk'. The student in this story is rather too much as I was.

'Bruce Lee' is an entertaining vignette of a dysfunctional but loveable family's barbecue and its aftermath. I won't forget the boy rubbing beer into his chest in order to put hair on it, and Frank is just like everybody's mischievous uncle. Mine was called John, and his speciality was embarrassing my aunt.

'Embroidered Poppies' is the history of a sheet. It's an original idea with the classic trajectory of a good short story; it works its way from an innocent beginning to a conclusion that is both a surprise and clincher. The reader is seduced by its sweetness, and then punched in the face.

'Murders and Murmurations' is the only piece in this collection which is an essay. It is an eccentric meditation by someone who sees the tenuous connections between things. It appeals to me because every year I bring up the young rooks that fall from the rookery in my garden, and it is true that 'birds.... have much to teach us about ourselves.' Members of the crow family are very clever and humorous, and even the sweetest natured sometimes have fits of viciousness.

'Bon Appétit' is an uncomfortable joke, and 'Blue' is an equally uncomfortable portrait of someone who is apparently clueless about what is going on in her life, what it all means, and how things are for other people. The reader feels deeply embarrassed for her, if not contemptuous. A story should leave you feeling something, even if it is as negative as that.

'Freedom, 2.0' is a cameo of situations that were not possible when I was young. A young woman is footloose in Rio de Janeiro, recklessly arranging assignations with unsuitable lovers via electronic media, putting herself into all sorts of danger without really knowing why. The anomie is reminiscent of the student's in 'I Climbed the Castle Mound'. These are the things we do when our lives are pointless.

'Anagnorisis' is an amusing reflection upon submitting things to books such as this. It contains advice that I often give to would-be writers; never give up on anything. Even your most terrible failures contain something that can be salvaged, something that may be useful, something that can be reworked. My first novel ended up as my seventh.

'Stranding' is perhaps the story that will remain with me the longest. It may even be a memoir. The flensing of a whale is not an event that most of us are ever going to see; you would have to be from one of the Scottish islands, or the Faroes, or Iceland. The dismantling of such a vast animal can only be imagined. We do not know why or how the whale became stranded, but it becomes a metaphor for all of us who are mysteriously stuck with no further choices, and are 'wondering how to leave'.

These pieces of work are a pleasure; I am glad that I had the opportunity to read them, and for that I thank *The Mays,* and wish it a long and creative future.

Louis de Bernières

Foreword

Being asked to write this foreword for *The Mays* brought me back to my time at Oxford in 2014, the year I decided to leave behind a fledgling career in the social sciences for the possibility of one in the literary arts. As an emerging poet, I found inspiration and companionship in past issues of *The Mays*, and thus am deeply humbled to be invited to preview an array of exciting and innovative voices for this current issue. What you will find within these pages, Dear Reader, are creative and artistic works which contain 'the full range of [human] emotions' ('emotional inventory'). I couldn't help but be drawn repeatedly to the poems, all of which display a keen attentiveness to the possibilities of form and experimentation. Some writers also powerfully address pressing themes that afflict our current cultural moment through poetry and prose which demand of the writer (and the reader) a courage not to look away. In sum, I find myself impressed and heartened by the beauty and lyricism in these pages, and hope you will join me in celebrating the success of these writers.

Mary Jean Chan

Editors' Foreword

"April showers bring May flowers."

Although this April has been unseasonably dry, *The Mays* once again unfurls its pages. This year, in XXVII, we offer you pieces that are experimental and serious, playful and reflective, saturated with colour and memory. Blue threads its way through the anthology like a river, fitting for a book which draws its contributors from the university towns of Oxford and Cambridge, situated on the banks of the Isis and the Cam.

A particular desire to revitalise the visual section of *The Mays* has borne rich and enigmatic fruit. For the first time, this year's anthology is accompanied by an online supplement, allowing us to feature video and sound art: you can find these digital works on our website (themaysanthology.co.uk).

Infinite thanks must go to Mark Curtis and Dr Mike Franklin, for their pearls of wisdom and their patience, which has been as boundless as the ocean. They have steered many a *Mays* through choppy waters and into harbour, and we hope they will continue to do so for many years to come.

Thanks too, must go to our guest editors, Louis de Bernières and Mary Jean Chan, for their generosity in giving their time and words to this edition of *The Mays*. Last but not least, thanks to our committee, who have ploughed valiantly through hours of meetings, dozens of spreadsheets and hundreds of submissions to bring you *The Mays*.

Many *Mays* have come before this one, and hopefully many more will come after it. Take a dip (or a long swim) in our modest tributary! We hope it will refresh, surprise and delight.

Elizabeth Huang and Eimear Ní Chathail

Sarah Brady
Anagnorisis

"Are you going to submit something?"

"Probably not. I used to write a lot when I was younger but I haven't written anything in ages."

"You used to write? What about?"

"Oh, nothing serious. Just some cringey teenager stuff."

"Come on, tell me. I'm sure it wasn't that bad."

"I can't even remember, really – I just know it was bad. Like, really bad."

"Oh, please. Even if it was bad, that doesn't mean it has to stay bad. No one's writing is good in the first draft. That's the point of a draft: you have to work on it. That's why artists sketch and why musicians rehearse. Do you think Michelangelo made David on his first try? Let's say your writing actually is bad. Maybe it's truly awful. The worst story that was ever written, even – if you don't try and improve it, it always will be. Writing a bad first draft is better than writing nothing at all. At least you can fix something which is bad. A writer is just an amateur who persevered. The most tragic thing in the world is all the books that were never written because someone was scared of being 'bad'. Perfectionism is the death of the creative spirit."

"I suppose you're right."

"As per. So, you'll submit something?"

"Maybe I will, yeah."

So, I go back to my room, sit down at my desk and open my laptop. Buried in the annals of a SanDisk memory stick, I unearth a relic — the likes of which mankind has not laid eyes on since the early twentieth century. My pulse quickens.

2011-08-25 11:58 /C:\\ Filename: Naruto Mpreg Fanfic DO NOT READ. docx\

Tanvi Roberts
emotional inventory

as simple as that! his mother asks
his one-year old face to simulate
angry crying happy surprised — in fact the full range of emotions
or at least the ones we stamp
words on as they hurtle back and forth
like trains. he obeys.
his baby-blank face unset
as yet by wrinkles twists into things
he's only heard of then snaps
back slick as an untangled
slinky. skin mud-smooth.
he thinks he knows these feelings now,
how to respond appropriately
as if on cue
so that when someone cuts across him
in traffic in say twenty years' time
or maybe pink sun shatters darkness
into shadows like a skater breaking ice
or perhaps he realises some leaving
is final unwave-like
he'll check his emotional inventory
and rifling through find the right one
every time

Angus Jackson
birthday
For Preti, Writing Together and everyone at HP Whitemoor

it is me awake in the beforetime when no one else is awake just me lying in bed awake and the time rushrushing and me stretching it eek making it longslow and eekeeking it. morning sound not yet beginning coocooing birds creakcreaking boards whishwhishing kettle but no is not nighttime no more not black cold hard no it is light peeppeeping round my curtains gentle gentle soft yes and night things no longer talking no not ruling time. it is my time this time this between time shh in bed before mum before school before chatter lunches joking bangbang noise and it is my time and it is specially my time this time this day because this daytime is my birthday day. hush hush hush must be shush and quiet and still in the dawn dirty light only you know only you must be with myself before am for others looklooking talktalking me. last year birthday day is too loud noise birthday too colour and cake and float-floating balloons and songs birthday all me myself everywhere I look me no escape. this year birthday day is secret shh shh no one knows it is mine me it is just shh shh you who knows don't tell shh shh just made by me like the worlds I make you where mum does not know dad is not there shh shh they cannot hear and no one can break them no shh. just me and her there myself and no parties no presents no boys no no NO shh shh shh mum comes down soon now I hear her now pat pat upstairs feet soon now she comes in and crackcrack my beforetime breaks my quiet my birthday day is not mine anymore not hers yours is everyones. but not this year no no not this year because I will hide me in myself just me and her and shh shh you I will hide from balloons whooshwhoosh and clattercrash plates and no boys no and mum knock knock she is here on my door breakbreaking into myself knockknocking down my door but I block no no from the others knock knock this year will be you her my day me and her and myself yes yes but mum knock knocks no no and I hunker down in bed yes with my yes her you and myself our refuge yes and there's no knock which can break me her us yes myself knock knock and yes I thinks yes I says to myself it is time yes for me to be yes now mum knock knocks in but no because yes I think this birthday day yes it is mine yes yes yes –

"HAPPY BIRTHDAY!!!"

Bruce Lee

We never went to church on Sundays, not like some of our neighbours. Sundays at our house were barbecue days. It was the one day of the week Frank could unwind, my mother said Frank wheeled the barbecue out of the garage at ten in the morning. He'd scoop the past Sunday's ash from the drum, into a plastic shopping bag I'd hold for him, and carefully stack lumps of charcoal in the middle of the drum, in a pyramid shape. He'd fill the gaps in the pyramid with chunks of fire-lighter briquettes that he'd crumble with his big hands.

"Go and get Uncle Frank a cold beer," he'd say, when he was finished.

And every Sunday I'd walk around the house, dump the bag of ash in the big bin, by the dog kennel in the back yard, and ask my mother to pass me a beer through the kitchen window.

She'd say the same thing, while she flipped the top off with a bottle opener.

"Bit young aren't you, son? Can I see some ID?" Then she'd smile and pass me a cold brown quart bottle. "Both hands," she'd say, "hold it with both hands."

People would start arriving just before lunchtime and Frank would light the fire and start cooking sausages, while everyone settled down in chairs on the front lawn. Some were wire chairs from the patio set and others were mismatched deck chairs, or fold-out camping chairs people brought with them. Everyone brought their own meat and drinks.

"Frank? Frank? Can we get the umbrella up, Frank? I don't want to burn."

Marjorie was at every barbecue I can remember. My mother called her a glamour puss.

Always dressed like she was going on a date or to a job interview, she said.

"It's only a barbecue, Marjorie."

"It's a cocktail party to me," Marjorie said, throwing her blonde head back, laughing before she lit a pink cigarette. "They're Russian," she told me once, opening the gold tin she kept them in. Marjorie also kept a small bottle of gin in her bag. "A gentleman never looks in a lady's handbag," she said, screwing the top of the bottle back on, and tucking it away.

"There you go, Princess Margaret." Frank said, clicking the top of the umbrella in place, and moving the sand-filled base by kicking it, until it blocked the sun from Marjorie's face.

"You're such a doll!" she said as Frank joined the other men by the fire.

"Your mother tells me your father's coming over today"

I nodded. He was. That was how today was different. My father was coming over to the house on a weekend. He preferred not to come, except sometimes when he drove up to town on his day off, to pick me up to go to the Drive-In. I liked going to the Drive-In. I liked going with him.

We'd drive in slowly till we found a free spot and he'd say, "What about here?" and I'd nod and he'd pull up and stop and pull up the handbrake, when the front tyres reached the top of the hump, so the car wouldn't roll forward, and the windscreen was filled with the huge white screen ahead. I sat in the front passenger seat, with my own speaker clipped to the window and could adjust the volume myself if I wanted to. Sometimes we'd talk. Sometimes we'd just sit quietly through the ads, waiting for the movie to start.

At the interval we'd walk back over the tarred humps, to the shop behind the projection room and buy hotdogs and chips. I fell asleep during the second half of most of the movies we went to see, but never a Bruce Lee movie. I could watch Bruce Lee all night, every night. I'd stretch my eyes open if I felt sleepy or roll down the window for some air. I wanted to be like Bruce Lee, I told my father. And he said that was good to know.

"Why's he coming today? Oh! God! Tell me it isn't your birthday. I haven't forgotten your birthday have I? Susan? Sue? Have I forgotten his birthday?"

My mother was holding a plate of lamb chops by the fire. She smiled and shook her head. Marjorie's panic turned into a wide smile. She laughed tossing her head back again and lit another cigarette.

"Boy, you had me worried you little bugger," she said, blowing smoke through her nose.

"Why is he coming?"

"To hang a poster in my room." I said.

"Oh," said Marjorie, "that's exciting."

"Bruce Lee," I said, "it's a Bruce Lee poster."

"I won't have a Chinaman hanging around in my house," Frank said.

Some of the men laughed.

"Oh, shut up, Frank," said Marjorie, "this is a private conversation."

"It's not your house," my mother said, while Frank put the lamb chops on the grill.

"Why don't you be a good girl and go and get me another beer?" Frank said.

Marjorie stubbed out a whole cigarette. "I'll get it!" she said, as she walked with my mother back into the house.

I got up to follow them when I heard a hoot and a car pulled up behind me. My father parked on the street and flipped the latch on the gate to open it. He walked down the drive towards the house, tilting his head back in a greeting to the men by the fire.

"Hey, son," he said handing me a wide paintbrush. "You want to show me where you want this?" he asked looking at the roll of paper under his arm.

When he was done, my father rubbed the poster with his hands and said, "Perfect."

"He's perfect," I said.

"Sounds like you want to marry him or something." Frank said standing in the doorway. His shorts were streaked with charcoal dust and grease, and his bare shoulders and chest were red from burning in

7

the sun. Bruce Lee was also shirtless, but he looked nothing like Frank. Frank had tufts of dark hair on his chest. There were small white shapes on his red skin where the links in his thick gold chain had blocked the sun.

"Every kid needs a hero, Frank," my father said.

Frank smiled. "See you're still driving that Jap-trap," he said leaning against the door post and crossing his bare feet. "Must have over a hundred thousand on the clock by now. Why don't you come down to the showroom sometime and I'll make you a good deal? We've got two brand new sports cars in. I brought one home last week; a real pussy magnet."

My father banged the lid down on the paste bucket with his fist.

"No thanks. She's going just fine."

"Suit yourself," Frank said.

"Who's she?" my mother asked squeezing herself into the room past Frank.

"We were just talking about the car," my father said.

"Oh, Frank you need to take the meat off the fire or it'll be over-done," my mother said.

"It's only a barbecue, Susan," Frank said, laughing as he walked away.

"You want to stay for a drink?" she asked my father, "Marjorie's here."

"No, thanks. I've got to get back," he said.

"Suit yourself," my mother said.

That afternoon was long and hot and Frank and the other men became more red-faced and drunk as it burnt on. After my mother tidied up she said she had a headache and was going to bed.

"Night all," she called, "don't stay up too late."

"I'll make sure he gets to bed," Marjorie said.

"You staying?"

"Yes, if that's okay? It's getting too late to drive back now."

Soon the other men started trailing off home.

"Looks like it's just you and me, Marjorie," Frank said.

"Time for bed I think," she said.

"Why don't you come and shake Uncle Frank's hand?"

Frank squeezed my hand hard, like he always did.

"Oh stop it, Frank," said Marjorie, "he's just a boy."

Frank chuckled, his eyes watering from the smoke, while he poked around in the coals.

"Here," he said, handing me a gold beer can, "have this. It'll put hair on your chest."

Marjorie tucked me in and I begged her to leave the beer can on the bedside table.

"Okay," she said, "but don't drink it. I will check in the morning." She smiled.

"He doesn't have hair on his chest," I said, staring up at the poster above my head.

"Not all men do," she said.

"Will I?"

"Give it time," she said. "Sleep tight."

When I was sure Marjorie had gone back outside I picked up the can and shook it like Frank did before he asked for another beer. I stood up, balancing on my pillow, slowly pouring beer in my hand and patting it on Bruce Lee's chest. Then I did the same on my chest and drank what was left in the can, before I buttoned my pyjama top and fell asleep.

It was dark when I woke. My head hurt. I stood up. My head was spinning. When I reached the passage I was sick all over the carpet.

"Christ!" Frank was standing at the door. He was naked except for his briefs. "What a mess!"

"Frank!" Marjorie got up and tied the waistband around her nightgown. "Come on," she said, taking my arm, "let's get you back to bed."

"What's going on?" My mother had woken up too. She seemed confused, like she was drunk. "What did you do, Frank?"

"Go back to bed, Sue," Frank said, "everything's okay. The boy's had a bad dream. Go back to bed."

"Are you okay?" Marjorie asked my mother.

"She's taken a sleeping pill," Frank said.

And Marjorie said, "Don't worry Sue, I'll clear all of this up. It's okay. Go back to bed."

My mother had to work the next morning but insisted I stay home from school. She asked Frank to keep an eye on me until she came home at lunchtime. Frank said he'd be out in the garage cleaning his car, so I went into the spare room where Marjorie had slept the night before. The bed was unmade and there was a dark wet patch on the carpet in the passage by the door. Marjorie must have gone early that morning. She'd left the gold cigarette tin on the bedside table, next to an ashtray with a single yellow butt in it. I took the tin back to my room, opened it and sat down on the bed.

"Yes, ha ha ha," I said, throwing my head back like Marjorie, with a cigarette in my hand. "Get me some more ice. Thanks, Frank. You're such a doll."

Uncle Frank stood in the doorway.

"Well, well," he said, "what have we here? You really are a little pussy aren't you?"

I looked at Frank but wasn't sure if I should answer or what to say if I did.

"Uncle Frank's going to make a deal with you," he said.

He sat down next to me and put his hands together in an upside-down pyramid shape. "I won't tell your mother about this if you don't talk about last night. Okay?"

I nodded. He stood up and put out his hand.

"Stand up. Let's shake on it, like men."

I stood up and he squeezed my hand so hard my knees bent.

"Your father could have done a better job," he said, widening his eyes and pushing his head forward to point at the black and white poster above my bed.

Bruce Lee's chest had sagged away from the wall.

"Looks like he's grown a pair of boobs," he chuckled.

And then he was gone.

Grace Richardson
Fall and Spring

The spring air post-day-time hush
Utters plushness of to be and be still.
I can and will un-spill myself of
Tread, and fallen will, that which
Impresses.
This, distressingly, is
Known as de-stressing — rather
Aggressively suggesting weight
Resides inside the coil's un-
Springing, and not its delicious
Career.

Katharina Friege
Still Life with Fruit Bowl

She picks a clementine from her mother's fruit bowl,
Slides a practised fingernail beneath its porous rind,
Peels back smooth skin to reveal the bitter pith,
Splits between her thumbs two hemispheres,
Just like that. —

You asked me what a haiku was,
I spoke of strict syllabic sentimentality
Too light to abide by the laws of gravity
Unless pinned down, it
Splits words into halfmoon segments, picks
Moments, fragments,
The gentle rustling of blossom-laden branches.

She savours the sweetness on her tongue,
The burst of colour, its bright disruption
Of November hues;
Sucks the juice from each carpel
With relish, with abandon. No shame
In being little sister to the mighty orange,
Innocent fruit born of rutaceous loins.

When the final citric crescent has disappeared
Between parted lips
She gets up,

slowly,

Pushes back her chair, shuffles to the bin
And throws away the orange peel.

Krystofer Mac?ie
Bon Appétit

Two doctors walk into an elevator. One says to the other: "Do you like riddles, Dr Winston?"

He's a young fellow.

"Medicine is always a riddle, Dr Seiskward," says the elder gravely.

"Well riddle me this: if I ate myself, would I disappear or double in size?"

The senior rolls his eyes.

"Where do you find this rubbish?"

"Just answer the question."

"One cannot eat oneself. Riddles are meant to be clever, not asinine."

"Are you always so rational? Use your imagination!"

The junior retrieves a pill bottle from his coat, unscrews the top and flings the neck into his mouth. The senior grunts in disapproval.

"Where did you get those?"

"Nicked them from the pharmacy," he giggles.

"You're a doctor, you should know better."

The lift halts. In walks a third doctor, older still.

"Staying perky, I see," he chuckles.

"Sure am!" snickers the junior. "You want some?"

"Couldn't hurt, I suppose."

He hands the man a couple of capsules.

"I thought you'd be more responsible, sir," gasps Dr Winston.

"It's only a small dose," he says, swallowing the pills.

The junior interjects.

"Do you want to hear a riddle, Dr Frederic?"

"You know, I'm rather partial to riddles. Let's hear it."

The junior coughs smugly.

"If you eat yourself, do you disappear or double in size?"

"Oh, well that's easy," exclaims Dr Frederic. "You disappear."

"I'm afraid not, sir. Your muscles would convert to fat and expand. But good guess!"

"I saw it with my own eyes, Dr Seiskward. Are you calling me blind?"

The junior laughs, although he soon realises it wasn't a joke.

"What do you mean?" he inquires.

"Oh, it's an odd story... Not exactly pleasant."

The other two exchange perplexed glances.

"I'm sure we can handle it," says the junior.

Dr Frederic eyes the young man carefully, before pushing the close button.

"Very well. I hope you have the stomach for it."

* * *

"It was back when I was shadowing Dr Ying. We had an obese Frenchman on our hands, called Gaston Glouton. The man was so big he could barely fit on the operating table.

"The procedure was simple: liposuction around the abdomen. Everything was running smoothly, when suddenly his heart failed. We tried everything to revive him. To no avail.

"Then the impossible happened: he woke up! It made no sense. He blinked, observing his bare organs with complete detachment. Then he glanced at us. It was like we'd disturbed him in his sleep.

"'Please relax,' said Dr Ying. 'Everything is under control.'

"But the patient pulled the pipe from his arm before Dr Ying could intervene. Seizing the defibrillator, Gaston rubbed the receptors together and pressed them against his naked right ventricle. In a violent spasm, his heart raced into action.

"'Voilà!' he shouted, sitting up. 'I'm 'ungry, get me sam food!'

"We were transfixed.

"He retrieved the tube from his abdomen and began sucking on it like a long straw. We watched as all the fat went sliding back along the channel. Within minutes he'd swallowed it all down.

"'Right, what's next?' he said, licking his greasy lips.

"'Next?' exclaimed Dr Ying.

"'Do I look full to you?' he growled, pointing to his stomach. 'I need meat!'

"Arming himself with a scalpel, he tied his sheet around his neck like a bib and dug straight into his left kidney.

"'Are you mad!' gasped Dr Galliano.

"'What? I only need one!' the patient snarled through mouthfuls of his own flesh.

14

"He tore into the organ with careful delectation, blood erupting in violent streams of red and purple. He then reached for his right leg and started ripping off the calf muscles.

"'I'm too fat to walk,' was his justification.

"But he didn't stop there. Once he'd devoured both inferior limbs, he moved on to his liver, an organ he found particularly delectable. He then gobbled up both feet as if swallowing two rather large pills, before slowly masticating his genitalia.

"His upper body is where things got confusing. He burrowed into his abdomen with both hands, sucking up his intestines like strands of spaghetti. He then crammed his right forearm into his mouth and gnawed his way up to the shoulder, before doing the same with the left. Devoid of the tools to manipulate his meal, he plunged his face into his chest like an animal, mangling his organs into an edible mush. He finally gobbled up his stomach – a paradox that still haunts me to this day!

"You can probably guess where it went from there. He crunched the rest of his bones between his teeth like breadsticks. Then his mouth became a kind of vortex, swirling with blood and saliva as it sucked his head into nothingness. All that remained was an odd digestive system, comprised of thirty-two teeth, an oesophagus and a faceless pair of lips. He nibbled on the food pipe, which formed an ever-tightening loop around his mouth, until his throat finally swallowed itself. There was nothing left of him after that. Aside from the bloodstains, of course."

* * *

"So there, Monsieur Glouton believed that by eating himself he would double in size. All he did was consume himself, until all was gone."

Dr Winston presses the open button in a panic.

The junior bursts out laughing. He takes a swig of the pill bottle, before handing it to Dr Frederic. They finish it between them, licking their lips feverishly.

"It's not working," grunts Dr Winston, punching the button repeatedly.

He walks to the entrance and tries parting the doors, to no avail.

"We're trapped!" he gasps.

He turns to find both doctors fixating on him with bright red eyes.

"Doctors?" he shudders.

They groan maniacally. And in almost perfect unison, their stomachs begin to rumble.

Lucy Tiller
On Wimbledon Common
after Frank O'Hara

On Wimbledon Common, palms pressed flat
against January air, elastic-bunched eyelids,
clouds unfolded wide as pillowcases (or

sails, or neat white steamed pocket-handkerchiefs
shaken out and tumbling along the unusual breeze)
we hurl ourselves down the untidy hill.

It is not so big as it used to be,
and the moans of the thick-set birds are cracked
and tinny. But it looks as though someone has burst

open a can of tinned peach-halves against the clouds,
glistening smudges curving in great syrupy crescents,
and dropped them as if the world was some corner-store

laundrette and every blast of the electric dryer
could fling peach-stained blouses into the air,
which was not air, which was air.

Hope Whitehead
i become a close acquaintance if not friend of queens' green

we learn that the council man has numbered each individual tree
along the ditch which used to be a riverbank
and would still be if it hadn't been for the year 1927.
question time: how are you going to stop pollution are you sure we
have bats have you seen can they park there have they been there too
long for rules did you really find trout —

i follow the ditch and try to work out if my ankle is sore

past tree number 49, which is a zelkova, i stagnate with the ditch
which is not a river anymore but still holds fog with the same
authority.
the zelkova, monotones the council man,
(somehow)
is immune to dutch elm disease.
the ankle, which is mine, throbs.

later and regardless of ankle the ditch is walked past again
and tree 49 which is not immune to darkness but still a zelkova
is somewhere to the left.
1927 pulls the river up and away from the hedgerow with a slight limp.
the fact of bats remains disputed
against the certainty of false river banks
fundraised for by well-meaning friends

Ben Vince
oh boy mother i am such a catch

the miles between us are just a membrane. I can cross them in a poem.
'Mad Girl in Love,' Melissa Lee-Houghton

the god stretches before me on the bed
diaphragmless, manure-ridden, clasping
hair clumps between unsavoury digits;
i'm tempted to dig my fingers in,
deep, truncate his magnificent thigh,
leave him a jigsaw one piece missing.
oh boy he's potent laying there,
spreading his tight, limbering arms
all dark spitting swan akimbo;
i'll crawl into bed with you,
baby, i'll pick you apart
like a carrion vulture.
      * * *
please avoid excessive hair
down sink and bathroom plugholes.
so i trim my pubic hair,
flush it down the toilet bowl.
call me sick or whatever.
i'll say what i fucking please.
      * * *
i am several layers of skin deep in this —
untoward detestable and murky;
prostrating myself before a poisoned body —
desire coming to collect me,
as if, on the shore, stranded by the docks

near an indiscriminate town,
harpooning lost lovers through the back.
        * * *

i am so full of love like a casket
for you and you both, it's malnourishing.
i sweep the bluebell scattered forest floor
for trinkets, containers for my large heart.
maybe i've been years on the run from it
or born miles from that lovely location.
        * * *

the japanese have started harpooning again
but no, darling, why don't we just sit here sucking
on each others' blowholes?
i didn't mean to bring it up but you're the one
kneading my leg fat as if it were whale blubber,
so don't look so startled.
        * * *

oh boy mother i am such a catch
i haven't even scratched the surface of it yet
been spinning silk webs for days even
i'm so proud that i love you and you love me
and that's not even the most of it now
swallowed a fever dream each night for the past week
tastes like salt whipped cream and floss
i could cough up half my love and drown someone
the more pungent the better i think
that's hardly all there is to say though
more of vases filled to the brim
less wetness in dreams of late that's natural
but there's still him there that chunk missing
and does he even know what i clasp in my woven hands
go ahead would you
tell him everything and more would you
it doesn't even scratch the surface.

Diana Paulding
Embroidered Poppies

Choosing a gift was a struggle for everyone who attended. There was a social obligation to buy, but when the postmen brought the smart cream invitations, the recipients knew that they would provide nothing but well-intentioned tat that politeness dictates cannot be thrown away. Mr and Mrs Henderson invite you to witness the marriage of their daughter, Esther Hope, to Thomas Francis Palmer Jr. The guests added it to the stack of other wedding invitations from college friends and cousins, and they panicked. They gambled upon a wine bottle stopper, useless in the age of screw-tops and a determination to leave no bottle unfinished. A set of cutlery in a velvet lined box that wouldn't fit in the drawer. A tablecloth, embroidered with poppies, to drape across the kitchen table and cover in cookie crumbs and coffee rings.

Thomas Francis and Esther Hope tried to find uses for each of the gifts in the early years of their marriage. They came back from their honeymoon in San Francisco and moved into an apartment near the flyover under which gangs met, where they could hear the lorries thundering past in the middle of the night and the recycling van burping with the weight of the bottles. For a while they played at married life. Dinner parties were hosted with colleagues and neighbours and the superfluous cutlery and the embroidered tablecloth. There were never enough seats. They brought in the garden furniture and moved the desk chair down from the study. Andrea from HR still had to perch on the arm of the sofa, her plate of chicken balanced on her knees. They laughed, they ate, they spilt red wine amongst the poppies. Andrea from HR threw salt on the wound and they vacuumed up the granules that dropped on the carpet.

After a while, a year or five, Thomas Francis and Esther Hope got bored of playing at married life and settled down to get on with it. They folded up the tablecloth and buried it without ceremony amongst tea towels and paper napkins and devoted their time together to watching television and keeping tallies on the washing up and forgetting to feed the cat. They compared the scratches that the cat used to remind and chastise them and fell asleep with him sprawled across their legs.

They ticked off the things that they were expected to achieve: promotions, a new house, a garden, the suburbs away from the flyover. The tablecloth was lost in the move but resurfaced a year later when a storm blew tiles off the roof. When they went into the attic to examine the damage they found a box that they'd forgotten to unpack sitting beneath the hole in the roof. The tablecloth was damp and stinking inside. A baptism in the washing machine and another poppy embroidered over the red wine stain, and they laid the sausage rolls and meringues on it at their little girl's christening. They called her Rose, not Poppy. They didn't want to name her after a tablecloth.

Rose grew up, as flowers and children do, and her class learned about castles. They made cardboard citadels with pipe-cleaner portcullises; she came home to suburbia and built a fortress. Her parents moved the chairs — they owned enough now — and Esther Hope draped the tablecloth over them and joined her in the muted light beneath its roof. Thomas Francis ducked the soft-toy-soldiers that his wife and daughter threw at him to defend the fort. They brought Rose orange juice and cookies with the fanfare of a banquet and mopped up the moat when the soft-toy-soldiers knocked over the cup.

Money ran tight as the economy stumbled. She needed fancy dress, so Thomas Francis found safety pins in the first aid kit and pinned the tablecloth around her, clipping leaves from the garden in her hair. Rose came back from the party seething because she'd been informed by Katy Harper in her fairy tutu that the Romans didn't wear embroidered poppies. There followed a discussion on historical accuracy and artistic interpretation and bullies.

Rose forgot about castles and remembered about the Romans, and she learned about Washington and Einstein and Parks, with whom she was proud to almost share a name. She had a stall at the science fair and Thomas Francis helped her cover it with the tablecloth. She set up pots of seedlings in varying stages of development. The mud stained the cotton. They scrubbed it out in the evening and talked about detergent and elbow grease and her first prize.

They covered her with it when they found her shot down in the front yard as she was leaving for school. Blood blossomed amongst the poppies. The blood stained the cotton. The gang members dispersed, disappeared, seeking their real target, and Esther found her on the lawn. She screamed and slapped her daughter's face in hope of some life, and Thomas Francis came out and sat down very suddenly on the grass. They covered her face and waited on the garden path for the too-slow emergence of sirens towards them. Her nose and her lips were visible through the fraying fabric.

Her coffin was covered in roses, but they threw the tablecloth away. They kept the bottle stopper and the cutlery, for they had not been covered in sausage rolls and meringues whilst Rose kicked her baby feet and burped at distant uncles, they were not blanket forts, they were not togas, they were not bruised by blood and stained too deep for cross-stitching to cover.

Dan Critchlow-Whitaker
Bunking

I miss smoking cigarettes
with you, behind the swimming pool.
While the other boys brushed bare skin, passed
each other like nothing,
like water,
we were sharing each other's breath.
Stomachs twisting, heads spinning,
lungs filled with something.

Then in my mother's bathroom scrubbing clean my fingers,
my sullied lips. Gargling saltwater
until I am the ocean
and you can bathe in me.

Alfie Robinson
Ode to Miniscule Frequency Words

At the very bottom of the overwhelmed sieve

Grains of silicate that'd sand your fingers
that no-one wants to hold

They are specialist terms that have become obsolete.

"Zeagonite"
Fool's-gold.

Lucy Tiller
Dissertation Research

Twelve metres from the car the water foams
away at the pebbles. Two pound coins
for two hours are toyed in the palm, the bright
sun which hangs just out of reach of the salt
spray keeping her untowelled toes
very nearly dry. We buy strawberry ice

from an untrodden café. My ice
is served by a lady whose lips foam
with waking. She unfurls her sore old toes
towards the cash register, thumbing coins.
Unrushed wind unsettles each lick with salt.
It slides in off the sea from the bright

edges of things, and the water shakes in bright
strips fanning out towards the sky. The ice-
cold sea is vague with misty blues, salt
fizzing through my cloud of hair, and foaming
with cold I unwind into life. Someone coins
the word unlistlessness. The tiny-toed

feet of the waves scuttle over my toes
bare, uncurling, flinging themselves brightly
onto the pebbles like polished coins.
Somebody skims one and it bounces twice,
delighted as it vanishes into the foam
and throws up water and the taste of salt.

The little clouds look they are salt-
streaked. With my own naked stirring toes
I find I can startle the fizzy white foam.
The greys and browns of the pebbles are bright.
There are no neutral tones here. Even the icy
greys of the grinning sea glimmer like coins

dropped by an unthinking god. Two five-pence coins
in my jeans' pocket are wrapped in salt,
with its slight and flicking hands. The ice-
cream shop, unattended, tiptoes
towards closing time. The last bright
smudges in the sky are dissolving into foam.

I wrap my toes in socks, and the salty
air catches my eyes like bright coins. The car
foams to life again. My fingers feel like ice.

Joanna Kaye
After

After: he drives off, that cliché of tyres screeching on tarmac. He turns on the radio. Does up his trousers, uses her cash to fill the tank. The taxi is waved down by another girl outside another club. He looks at her legs in the rearview mirror.

After: she starts to run, and then her lungs are burning, and then she is sick. She collapses between two parked cars. She sends a message: please help me, but no one does. A car passes, and she thinks about crawling out into the road and letting it hit her.

One week after: he drives past her in the taxi. He does not even recognise her, but catcalls anyway.

One week after: the HIV-preventative pills make her vomit. She thinks she looks grey. She brushes her teeth until her gums are bleeding and scrubs her skin raw and still the smell lingers, until it is just hers, and his, and the two are the same, and he has stolen her and left himself behind. Her father says, half of the words choked on the buffering video call, that she must feel this, and she wonders if he is feeling it too, as he says that her life might be a before and after, hinging upon this singular, devastating moment, and she wonders if his life will be too. And she is free-falling, faster, faster, faster than terminal velocity.

She thinks about dying, thinks that this is maybe it, wonders if someone were to hold her tight, too tight, until she can no longer breathe, she might not shatter.

One month after: he lies in bed with his wife. She tells him she likes it when he misses the night shift. He touches her skin with fingernails that have clawed at someone half his age.

One month after: she holds onto the jagged fragments of what she can remember. There is a pleasure in that, in puncturing the same scabbed wounds, over and over, in feeling a wound heal and then break open once more. She craves some visible trace of what happened, a deep black bruise fading through the greens and yellows and greys and then eventually into nothing at all.

Four months after: he visits his mother. She looks at him as all mothers do, eyes glazed with the sheen of something irrevocable and utterly unconditional. He kisses her forehead, tells her he loves her, with the same lips that released a nauseating purr of non-consensual delight.

Four months after: she imagines the therapist split in two: the rapist. His encouraging half-smile becomes a leer, his handshake a threat, his sterile office the taxi. Insurance companies will cover the losses of a robbery, but when he ruined her, they didn't give her anything. Instead, she pays minute-by-minute for a stranger to listen, until she drowns in that blank hour and the illusions she builds. So, she runs. Back to her family, thousands of miles away, a fourteen-hour haze of tears and tepid packaged food and

Six months after: he takes his grown-up daughter for a birthday dinner. They talk about the boy that broke her heart and it breaks his too. He drives her home himself, because he does not trust those cabs on the street. He drives past the girl but does not even notice her, because his hand is on his little girl's leg this time around, tender this time, protective this time.

Ten months after: they are drinking, laughing, all men, and there is no talk of rape. It is his unacknowledged secret, a splendid paradise that would be marred by discussion.

the feeling of being chased. She wonders why no one asks, why they do not care, why their worlds continue exactly the same when hers cannot. Headlines forgotten, new ones outshining them; old jokes returning, sex still blasé. Six months after: she feels a buzzing glow on her skin, something like peace or God or just sunshine. She is happy, but she is also bruised: by the taxi driver, by the inviolable taboo of talking about appalling things, by the boredom of being enslaved to the same pain. She resents her wish, chokes on it, as she prays for a saviour. Strong, comforting, protective. Male.

Ten months after: they are drinking, laughing, all women, and someone shrieks, 'would you rather be murdered or raped?' and they unanimously agree, rape, yes, definitely rape, a thoughtfulness to their thoughtlessness, a mockery of humans ravaging other humans, of men ravaging women, of people being broken, just because they themselves have not been. She thinks: he did not even give me the choice.

A year after: he renews his taxi licence, another year, another validation for the things he does on worn seats. Hollywood is being purged, but no one will hear if she does not speak, so he does not even think of her.

A year after: the date scours her, bristly, throbbing, and the shape of the feeling is unfamiliar, entirely new. She does not leave her bed, and enjoys the clichéd triumph of it, of being paralysed by a half-forgotten horror. The jagged fragments are still in her pockets, and when she removes her hands, they are stained red, fattening scarlet dewdrops emerging from those old scars. Except her hands are in fists now.

Forever after: the hunted are the hunters now.

Forever after: the hunted are the hunters now.

Evan Silver
Murders and Murmurations

Last fall, I went backpacking in the Adirondack Mountains of upstate New York. I woke up early one morning to sit by a lake and watch the sun rise. I sat on a rock at the edge of the lake and scribbled some notes and sketches in a little journal. I marvelled at the simultaneous stillness and non-stop motion of the lake, the billions of molecules of water moving with verve and intensity, and yet the shocking quiet of only rarely heard vibrations: the creaking murmurs of bark, the water lapping gently against a rock, the rumbling in my eardrums. My own beat.

I write, "An argument for conformity? ... A flawless natural machine of movement and repetition." No selves to speak of, only a whole comprised of its unselfish parts. Some kind of essential beauty.

A bird swoops and parts the sea. Glides against the water, makes a sound like shuffling a deck of cards. We sit in the rushing stillness.

A murmuration of starlings is like an aerial ballet of deftly coordinated movements. Thousands, even millions of birds consume the sky like a swirling, shapeshifting ocean, mysteriously twisting into dizzying quicksilver formations. The effect is godlike, as if the birds are magnetised to the invisible currents of life energy that permeate the universe.

No selves to speak of, only a whole comprised of its unselfish parts.

Scientists have only begun to make sense of the natural phenomenon. What they have found is that murmurations are brought about when a predator such as a hawk or a peregrine falcon is near. The flock's movement is an evasive manoeuvre: the enormous mass of birds twists and shifts in every direction to disorient the predator. The starlings find safety in numbers. Even birds that are far from the site of danger sense the shifts in movement and fly in unison with the collective.

New technology has allowed humans to track this process of coordinated movement by recording it, slowing it down, and analysing its discrete parts. It recalls for me another history: when in 1892, race-horse owner Leland Stanford hired photographer Eadweard Muybridge to settle the controversial debate on whether or not all four feet of a horse were ever off the ground at the same time while galloping. Muybridge's stop-motion photography — the advent of modern technology — proved that horses did in fact have all four hooves off the ground while running. Where the human eye had failed to perceive — as well as, consequently, the artists who painted horses at a trot with one foot always planted on the ground - science could illuminate the unseeable (or, more accurately, unperceivable) mysteries of nature in motion.

In the case of murmurations, scientists have found that each starling is reacting to the birds nearest, and the overall movement of these intelligent clouds is a result of a series of nearly instantaneous close-range reactions. Like water molecules pushing up and colliding against one another in a lake. One bird only affects its seven closest neighbours, causing a massive ricochet effect.

One of my favourite theatre exercises is something called flocking. In this exercise, a group of actors will assemble in a mass (i.e. a flock, not a line) behind an initial leader. The group will mimic the movements of the leader as she moves through space, changes tempo, shapes, and levels, until the group organically rotates through space, establishing a new leader at the front of the flock. The group listens and follows as leaders shift. The ensemble moves in (almost) unison, the culmination of (nearly) instantaneous close-range reactions.

The exercise requires intense focus and listening. It requires a kind of selflessness, a total willingness to give yourself over to the group dynamic, to conform. There is no hierarchy, only a gentle shapeshifting between leaders and listeners travelling through space to create scenes, shapes, movements. In larger groups, it is very easy to lose track of the leader who began the motion. So you follow those bodies closest to you.

I feel powerful in these groups. Not as an individual, not in terms of my self, but in terms of being part of something larger, and more important, than myself. There is power in being a fleck of black in a murmuration. A drop of blue in a lake. A listener in the ensemble of humanity.

Not very long ago, we could not see that the horses were midair. We could not tell how the starlings listened, how their flocks cast ethereal shapes in the sky. There is a capacity in science and technology to illuminate natural truths.

However, the limits of human knowledge are boundless. Perhaps there is a truth to the gut feeling: that this is something much larger than ourselves. Do the gods speak through the birds? Do starlings fly through invisible currents of life energy like pathways in cosmic river systems?

Terms attached to groups of specific animals — a "murmuration" of starlings and a "murder" of crows — are poetic inventions that date back to the fifteenth century. Many of these words, called "terms of venery" or "nouns of assembly", made first appearances in John Lydgate's Debate Between the Horse, Goose, and Sheep (1440) and Dame Juliana Barnes' The Book of Hawking and Hunting (1486), otherwise known as The Book of St. Albans. Whether or not Lydgate and Barnes coined the terms themselves or reflected the common parlance of their day is unknown. Regardless, their books were circulated widely. Some of the terms have endured the test of time, while others (such as a "pitying" of turtledoves and an "ostentation" of peacocks) have not fared so well.

Many of these collective nouns reflect actual animal behaviour. An "exaltation" of larks refers to the way a skylark flies high into the sky while tweeting its pleasant song. Perhaps "murmuration" is meant to describe the way the starlings chatter about as they begin roosting each evening. But the starling's voice is hardly notable and sounds more like an ecstatic jabbering than a gentle murmur. I am more inclined to believe that "murmuration" is a poetic reflection on the way flocks of starlings undulate and ripple through the sky. A kind of whisper shared across an ocean of birds like a high-speed game of telephone.

The word "murmuration" was initially synonymous with "flock". It is not until very recently that it has come to refer more specifically to the phenomenon in question. This shift can possibly be traced back to a Huffington Post article written in 2012, which used the word "murmuration" to describe the "thousands of tiny starlings (birds) collectively flying and swirling about" — murmuration as an act. With about thirty-six thousand "likes" and who knows how many reads, a new meaning was murmured, and it rippled through the collective human imagination by word of mouth. A bird shifts in direction and the rest follow: this is how language contorts through time.

The collective noun seems to subsume its discrete parts. A "flight" of stairs is nothing beyond the collective. What can you do with a single stair? With a multitude of stairs, you can literally transcend ground level and become suspended mid-air. Stairs permit flight.

Perhaps we might begin to think of ourselves more like stairs.

"Murder" seems an unfortunate name for the crows, but it's unsurprising given the frequent association between crows and death. Predatory scavengers that will eat practically anything, they are known to make homes around dead bodies, battlefields, and cemeteries. Some people believe that crows circle in large numbers where animals or people are expected to die shortly.

However, in many cultures, crows are revered as deeply intelligent and compassionate creatures. In Blackfoot Indian lore, it is said that, a long time ago, the crow was the same size and shape as it is now, but was the most colourful of all the birds. In fact, every other bird was solid black as the crow is now. One by one, the other birds came to the crow asking for a colour, and the bird obliged. Eventually, the crow had only brown left, until he gave even that away to the lowly sparrow. As he had given away all of his colours, the crow now had no colour at all, and was black. The Blackfoot Indians have deep reverence for the infinite generosity and selflessness of the crow.

The 14th Dalai Lama reflects on the murder of crows that came to roost at his parents' home around the time of his birth. He notes that this is of particular significance because of similar events that occurred at the birth of the First, Seventh, Eighth and Twelfth Dalai Lamas. According to Tibetan Buddhist history, the night after the birth of the First Dalai Lama, bandits broke into his family's home. The parents fled from the scene, leaving the child behind. When they returned the next day, they found their son under the protection of a crow. This crow eventually revealed himself to be the protective deity known as Mahakala.

The association between crows and death is complicated by the notion that life is circular. A crow might be a harbinger of birth just as easily as death. Perhaps it should be unsurprising that cultures that believe in death transcendence (e.g. a transition into a new realm, karmic rebirth) have a reverence for the crow that death-fearing people do not.

Crows memorise garbage truck routes to ensure a daily feast. They leave nuts in the middle of the road and wait for passing cars to crack them open. When a crow is killed in a farmer's field, the flock will change entire migratory patterns so that no crows fly over that plot of land for years. Crows memorise faces; they keep friends and hold grudges.

Whether or not they are gatekeepers to another spiritual realm is yet to be determined by fancy stop-motion science equipment. What we do know is that the birds — whispering secrets on telephone lines and Hitchcockian jungle gyms — have much to teach us about ourselves. And perhaps it is our fear of how much we do not know — or, arguably, our fear of death, especially the death of the self — that keeps our focus eye-level, staring forward into the future with little consciousness for the mysteries in the sky. One step at a time.

Jerome Lim
Bell Peppers

The peppers are bright green; they hang innocently on the branch;
the peppers gorge themselves silly; their fleshy chambers bloat with sunlight;
the peppers listen through their wiry roots, as littered leaves whisper about
the inevitable fall of everything; the peppers hear of teeth & knives; fear & heat
ripens the peppers—some red, some yellow; the yellow peppers are plucked
by soft fingers; they scream their sunlit insides out; the hornworms describe
to the reds how the yellow peppers are eviscerated with knives, claim the yellow
peppers are naturally inferior & deserve to die; the red peppers believe
the innocently green hornworms; untouched, the red peppers hoard sunlight
& gorge further; the last yellow peppers hang on the end of the branch,
furthest from the soil's gifts, & shrivel up; the hornworms begin to devour
the fat red peppers alive, who scream their sunlit insides out; the yellow
peppers release pheromones to protect themselves; the red peppers demand
asylum at the end of the branch; the yellow peppers, craving sunlight, leave
them to die; the hornworms ripen into moths & fly away; for a while there is
peace among peppers; the reds & yellows make out in their wooden cloisters,
propagating bright green offspring; peace ripens the peppers—some red,
some yellow, & one orange; the orange pepper declares himself the chosen
capsicum, & the other peppers inhale his messages through open stomata;
for a while there is peace among peppers, but they argue over the exchange
of nutrients; soon the orange pepper grows overripe, shows signs of falling,
& the nascent peppers fear the second hornworm invasion; when spring
transpires the orange pepper falls majestically; soon the other peppers follow;
they stare at blue sky from beds of soil, & dream of becoming bright green.

Night Wanderers
Grace Crabtree

Mycology
Anna Dobrowolski

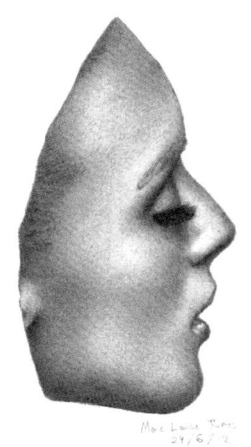

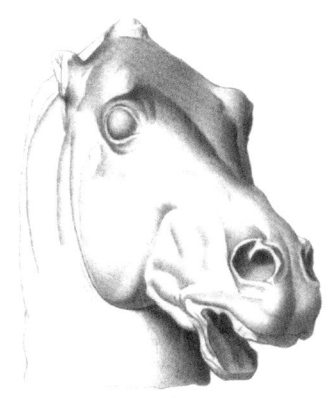

Untitled #1 (top)
Untitled #2 (bottom)
Marie-Louise James

2. tracing

to sleep on it
Ruari Paterson-Achenbach

Everyone I have ever slept with on Tinder (minus the one I actually liked)
Anonymous

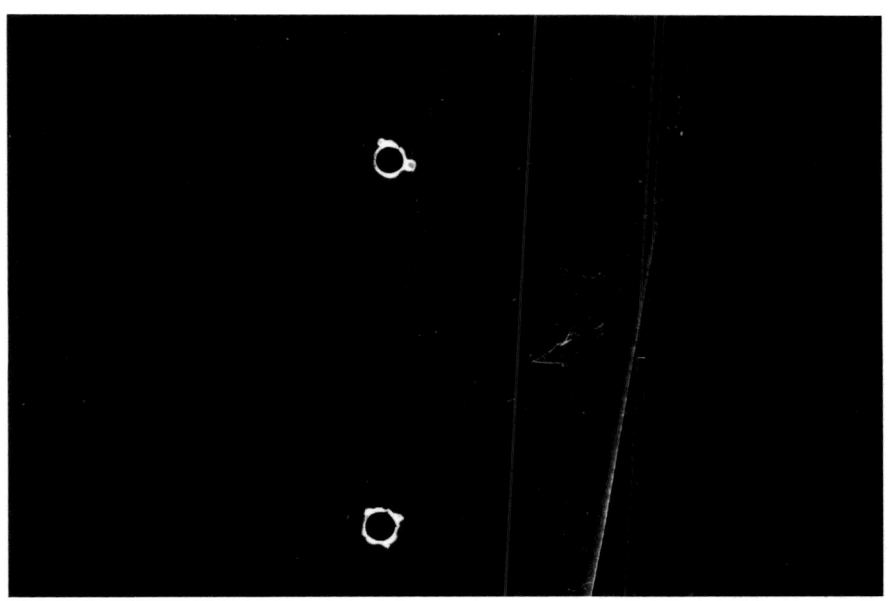

Eccentricity
Thomas Davidson

Untitled #1 (top)
Untitled #2 (bottom)
Mathias Gjesdal-Hammer

Fisherman's Bastion
Matthew Seccombe

Lightbulb Moment

The sun goes down around four nowadays

and the bulbs of the streetlamps warm themselves slowly on the darkness.

They ought to be overwintering with the onions and the tulips pocketed beneath the soil

Seems wrong somehow them being so tall

.Bulbs.

Sumptuous Speckled

Vielleicht haben die Deutschen hier Recht

.Glühbirne.
—Glow Pear—
...

harbouring light

46

Lightbulb Moment
Jenny O'Sullivan

Untitled
Clover Godsal

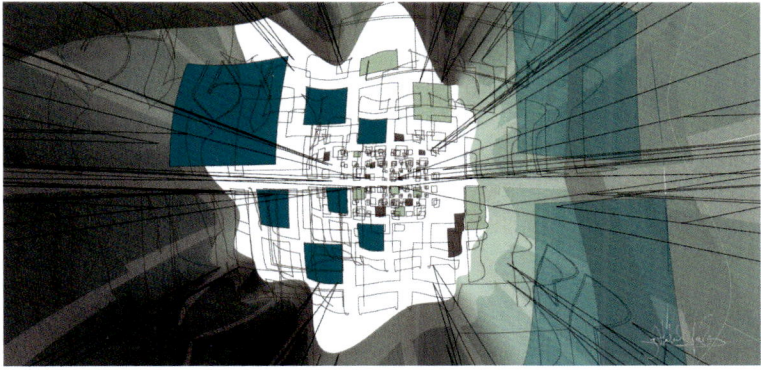

Polytopes and space (de)construction
Georgios-Spyridon Athanasopoulos

49

Pina
Esme Garlake

Lyda
Esme Garlake

Untitled #1
Alisa Santikarn

Untitled #2
Alisa Santikarn

Revolution and Rubble
Riley Kaminer

Thinking of you
Nesem Petek Ozbey

Untitled
Catherine Macnaughton

Portrait of an Artist as a Young Woman
Zoë Matt-Williams

Lloegyr
Mary Gatenby

The Whale
Mary Gatenby

Blocks & Bins
Levin Pfeufer

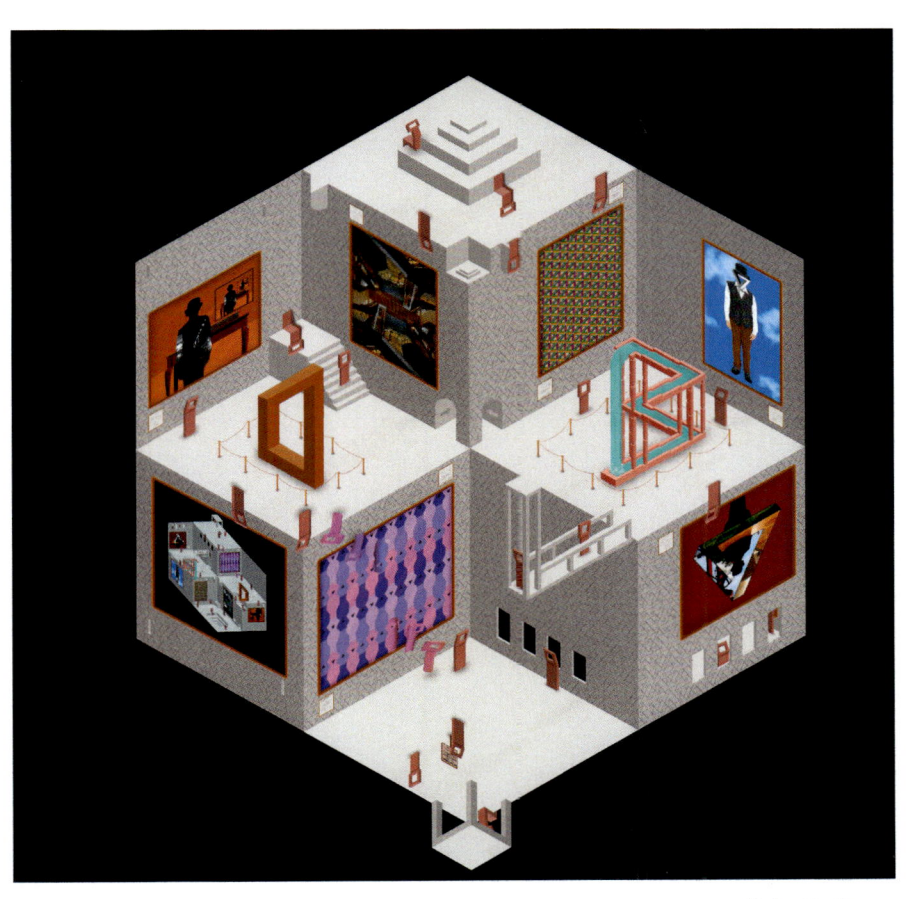

Impossible Gallery
Zébulon Goriely

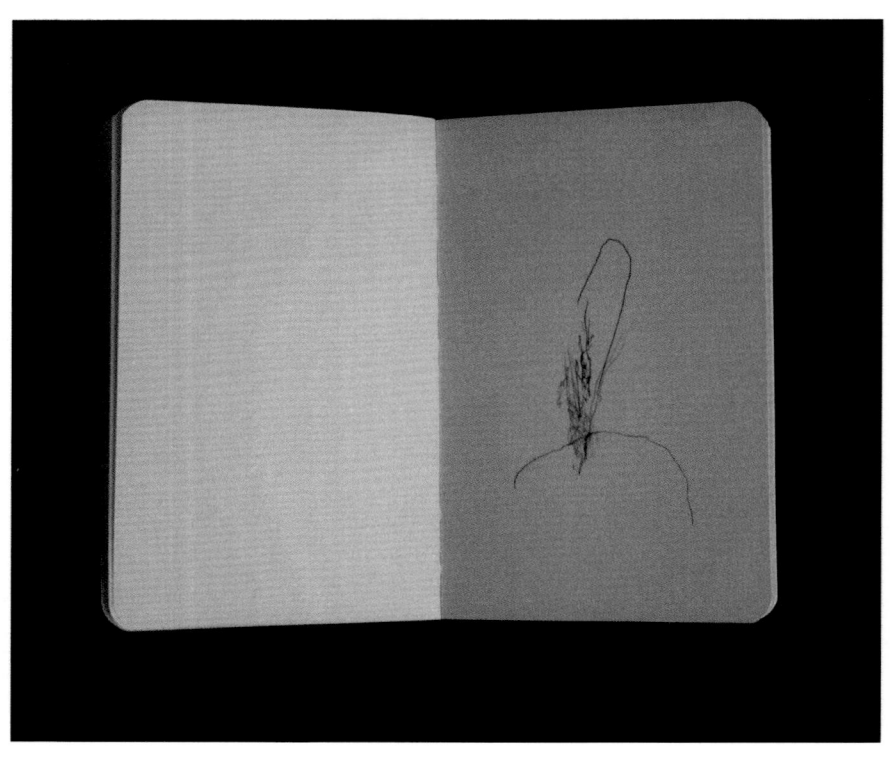

The Sensate Travels of a Soma #1
Evelyn Whorrall-Campbell

Vida Adamczewski
Magpies

1
I saw one once, on the road. Feet in the air.
Blood sodden and slicked onto the tarmac.
Wet feathers splitting into licks.
A few nipped blades of grass by its side;

They grieve, you know. A pair of sorrows
Swooping over each other
One then one they settle
To peck the earth.

2
a conventicle
a congregation
a murder
a tiding
a tittering
a charm
a gulp

3
The length of the magpie's tail indicates social rank.
During the breeding season, the hen can be identified by her bent or
damaged tail feathers.

4
A clutch of blue speckled eggs.
They sit there, growing, silently.

At the end of the branch, he stands vigil.

5
Most magpies are spinsters,
They stick together like book clubs.

They are noisy too. Hard to get a word in
Edgeways with all that chacker chacker chit chat

About that little old lady
With the long black coat and the hats.
We nod knowingly. Like them,
She keeps things. Accumulating trinkets.

They settle on windowsills, peering.

I have an unfortunate habit of inching the windows open over night
(I overheat. You add: Probably hormonal. We all nod.)

In she bustles, neat and prim as those women who iron their towels.

I trace the red rut on my fourth finger.

A flurry of kleptomanic winks
And a ring carried off like a trick.

6
A bad rep for nicking glitz
Because of that one bird
In Rochdale.

7

In spring, the local population of Magpies
gather to resolve social and territorial disputes.
These are called parliaments.

Here, the assembled Magpies
Identify their partners. Soon after
Plots of land will be allocated to each couple.

The Magpies, of course,
Will scatter if you approach

Valk Fisher
Connective Tissue

I. September 27, 2018

SENATE JUDICIARY COMMITTEE HEARING ON THE NOMINATION OF BRETT M. KAVANAUGH TO BE AN ASSOCIATE JUSTICE OF THE SUPREME COURT, DAY 5, FOCUSING ON ALLEGATIONS OF SEXUAL ASSAULT

II. Duality

It's ripping season.
Or so the surgeon says, the knee is a hinge with only one degree of freedom, structurally
unsound for directional shift, meaning, your anterior cruciate ligament has torn.
The MRI shows an injury in Grade 3, diagnosing the tear as complete.
You picture: behind the patella's turtle shell, the newly barbed ends in a bloody rift.

It – the world – would split
was one Poet's conclusion to a question: what would happen
if a woman spoke the truth about her life?

Yours is a tear that's fashioned for its times. Fallout from things that continue to split lands on one of only   two   sides.

III. Naproxen

She testifies in the tone of your prescriptions for pain. That sounds good. That would be great. Does that work? Do you mind? Sorry. I'm used to being collegial, so. Whatever is your preference.

You know it. You've taken it too, smeared yourself in enteric coating until becoming
slightly sweet on the tongue, safe for soft inner linings, anti-inflammatory.
The pundits like her. She's pretty credible, pretty likeable, pretty believable.
Because she's been resurfaced for swallowing?

IV. Dirty laundry

A president is on Twitter again. He wants to know why, why didn't somebody call the FBI 36 years ago? This the newest in a series of closed questions.
In other words said, that dog. Crazed crying lowlife. Too disgusting, and fat! Miss Piggy bleeding badly, blood coming out of her wherever. These things soak in your mind's spin cycle but will not wash out clean. Trending power words soil. An actual Reckoning might involve whip-yielding witches, bleeding badly.
Your innermost parts come undone with the season, cooked inside like pulled pork.

V. A history of shame and the androgyny of abuse

The Committee has the same question. Why have you held it to yourself all these years?

How far back is it helpful to go?
Five-year-old you and dad are at the beach. You are to stay on the sand. He swims.
From the water a stranger, Come in! Don't be scared. Do you like to swim? You do.
You look to ask dad. His eyes are covered in goggles.
He finds his daughter's back held too tight against heaving breasts. You can't access the details, but remember his furor. And then this small voice:

I'm sorry, I'm sorry, please don't tell Mom, I'm so, so sorry.

VI. Is all outrage made the same? And allowed questions?

I categorically and unequivocally deny the allegation: a national disgrace, a circus, a calculated political hit. I busted my butt. Got into Yale College. Got into Yale Law School. Going to church was like brushing my teeth. This is who I was. This is who I am. Use your common sense. What rings true? What rings false?

SENATOR AMY KLOBUCHAR (D, MN): *You're saying there's never been a case where you drank so much you didn't remember?*

It's, you're asking about, you know, blackout. Have you? Have you?

VII. ~~Taking~~ Reconstruction

The problem with things that come apart is what to make of the severed pieces.

Your anterior cruciate ligament cannot be re-tied. The treatment is in the taking: fresh graft carved from living flesh, forced through bone-hollowed tunnels.

This is reconstruction.

VIII. Economics of Redistribution

Your friend is afraid to date women. The dynamics are all distorted. Men are rapists until proven decent. Consent contracts, really? Aren't we overrationalising a primal thing?

A friend slaps him with her furious fist:

Do Not. You do not get to say that.

Who fits the brace? Meaning, who must wear it?

IX. Desire of a Mad Woman

In a dream you wander in a white-walled space with a brace on the place your jaw comes to a hinge. You scream from within for a pivot. Want of words rises like a balloon in your throat that wakes you with its rubber burst.

You see. The pathology was at the root.

In the bruised purple morning it is clear. All along what you've wanted is to come unhinged.

Poet's note:

The Poet referenced in section II is Muriel Rukeyser, the lines "It – the world – would split. / This was one Poet's conclusion to the question of what might happen / if a woman spoke her life's truth." references her poem 'Käthe Kollwitz'.

Untitled
Lisha Zhong

Danielle Silverman
Albany

I may have kissed the window of the airplane
as we flew over the Hudson.
I knew I did not cross the Atlantic
for a processional promenade down a highway in America
for nostalgia and a side of fries.
Red, white-stained yellow, and blue.
Although it wasn't blue this time of year,
and even as I came to Albany,
my thoughts were drawn
to that huge grey egg they stuck on the plaza of the state buildings.
And how your father worked at the capitol,
And your mother in agency building
number three.

Albany,
you smell of egg sandwich lunch breaks.
Albany,
I may have kissed you anyways.
Albany,
I never found you as a family friend,
but it was you skating over the watered down courtyard,
sipping hot cocoa out of melted plastic cups.

Grey Albany, for you were not always grey,
sometimes you were golden.
Even though they paved you in Georgian marble,
you were stained by some exhale from a smoky hush,
the rain of firework residue,

and exhaust from those Canadian oil trucks.
And when I remembered you in white, I forgot.
That you didn't like the way I chopped the yellow bell peppers,
or the garlic,
or the onions.

Grey Albany, you are no rival to New York,
and you tried so hard to be.
You spilled a bit of black coffee
on your black sweater,
and smoked your cigarettes
on the windowsill and watched the ash
fall until it hit the concrete.
You go to Shabbos at seven, drag races at twelve,
and wake up in the arms of Justice, who took her blindfold off
and wondered at what point she picked up the scales.

Neoclassical child, I wish I never romanticized you.
I wandered through your legs of Corinthian columns
hoping to look up and find some Parisian
grotesque.

I wanted to walk home
from the building I watch every night,
but you called me a cab.
And I watched in the rearview mirror,
as the lights turned from blue to purple to green.

Albany,
I'm glad you drink gin now.

Elle Lavoix
Freedom, 2.0

There is so much freedom in youth.

You meet Diego on Tinder. He is not like the guys you date back home. He is local, a sexy little Carioca beach boy who freely admits to being jobless, spending his days bumming around Copacabana and rolling joints for his mother. You refrain from asking him how he earns his money.

You have free tickets to all the matches, so you invite him to a Brazil match. Before the game you go to a street side drinking hole, one he has carefully chosen for the quality of its refrigeration. You have only been dating for two hours and you already know how important it is for his cerveja to be bem fria. Never warmer than 9 degrees.

To your great shame, you arrive at the game after the first whistle. You wait for a stop in play, then hurriedly lead him to the front row seats, ducking down, squeezing past hairy knees and tip toeing over sticky puddles of beer and soda. At the game he is raucous, jumping to his feet and hurling obscenities at the opposing team whenever there is a foul. You shrink in your seat and hope the officials who knew your father have not understood that this cara is with you. You are secretly rooting for the other side, but you also know that if Brazil loses, the men here will be white with anger.

Between two rowdy displays of discontent, he lights up a cigarette.

"I don't think that's allowed here," you point out in vain. He looks at you like you're a killjoy.

When Brazil does win, Diego fervently joins the thousands of people pouring out onto the streets belting out Brazil's national chant, Eu sou brasileiro, and you follow him lackadaisically. When the celebrations end, Diego finally takes off the nylon flag he's been wearing like a cape and the two of you head to a night restaurant. He orders carne seca com aipim and rambles about his past life as a teacher. You listen and nod, but deep down you are skipping through this city, the cidade maravilhosa, wearing a bubble gum pink skirt and holding your dad's hand as he leads you through the gnarled mango trees to the wide open sea.

In front your Airbnb, Diego pulls you towards him into an insistent kiss that tastes of stale cigarettes and fried cassava. You debate whether to invite him upstairs or not. His body does feel nice in your arms — maybe a bit wiry — and at this stage, saying yes seems a hell of a lot easier than saying no.

As you lead him upstairs, you realise that you have already done this six times.

Freedom must be living without fear.

Upstairs, he spends so much time between your thighs pleasing you that you regret not having timed it. Later, you will affectionately record this marathon of Brazilian lovemaking in your diary. He lets himself out of the apartment in the early morning, tucking your hair behind your ear and whispering goodbye.

In the afternoon you laze around on the couch, sinking your toes deep in the woolly white rug and sipping mango juice. Out of sheer curiosity, you open Tinder and browse the other profiles. You stumble upon the well-built Bruno, 28, three kilometres away. In his first photo, he's wearing a red sweatshirt and standing in front of a dizzying mountainous landscape that gives way beneath him, laughing as he places his hand on a zip line. In the next photo, he's at Carnival, drinking beer and wearing a Panama hat, surrounded by friends decked out in glitter, feathers and flowers. He looks self confident. You wonder if he's a good dancer. You hesitate for a second, then swipe right.

That's what freedom is. Choice.

He messages you immediately. Oi Eva! Tudo joia?

Tudo, you reply. E contigo?

Tudo.

A pause.

Are you free tonight?

You exit the app and head to the shower.

From the vents in the wall you can hear angry chanting from faraway streets. The city, like all of the Soccer Cities, is caught up in Brazil's newborn political implosion. Sexy Diego is an avid protester, showcasing his fury at the government and at FIFA through handmade cardboard signs. You yourself have known since childhood just how corrupt the world of elite football is, but you would never say this out loud.

Football is what brought you to Brazil as a child. Your father worked as a manager at Maracanã stadium in the two years leading up to the America Cup. Your father loved the beautiful game, the lively beaches, the sultry rhythm of samba music. You sensed he also loved Brazilian women, though your child-like suspicion never crystallised into an accusation. Your mother, on the other hand, had less love for Brazil and its thong-clad women. Early on, you were taught that a woman's respectability is directly proportionate to the amount of fabric covering her body.

By the time you exit the shower, your toes lovingly tucked into fluffy white slippers, five notifications from Bruno have arrived.

Where did you go?

Are you there?

Then, thirty minutes later: Hey, I'm free tonight at 10pm. Meet me at this place. I'll be there with my friends. He sends you a pin to a sports bar in a neighbourhood you have never set foot in.

You imagine yourself crossing the city after dark in a potentially dicey Uber to meet this unknown man and his five male friends in a bar which will most likely be dodgy and filled with drunk football hooligans.

That's what freedom is. Going wherever, whenever.

You try to strike a playful tone in order to reject the offer. That's very late!

Really? What time do you usually go out?

You don't answer.

But the next day, you agree to meet him on Ipanema beach in the afternoon. You remember Ipanema as a leafy seaside neighbourhood filled with tropical almond trees, small dogs and gelaterias selling açai. But as you arrive, you see stocky buildings and limping electric cables, giving way to a favela creeping up and over the hillside, its hastily built brick buildings crushing into each other under loads of drying laundry.

You easily find Bruno in the crowd. He's leaning back in a folding yellow beach chair with a satisfied smile on his face, wearing tight-fitting red bathing trunks hiked up to his crotch to maximise his tan. Snake tattoos wind down either side of his shaved torso. His right hand is running through his hair and the other is nurturing a cheap can of beer. Instead of facing the ocean, he's facing the outdoor showers and the women playing futevôlei.

He spots you and unfolds another chair for you. You slide into it, chatting in what you hope is an easy-going and disengaged fashion. In reality, you are self-conscious of both your whiteness and your prudish European bikini. A girl whose left shoulder is covered in gothic tattoos and who has jet-black hair hanging down to her waist saunters to the shower. She moves around the shower like a kitten purring. She looks like she's 17.

Bruno watches her through his fake Ray Bans, his lips slightly parted. You spot a trace of saliva in the corner of his mouth.

You discreetly angle your chair towards the sea. The beach is crowded, the sky is bright blue and the waves are shoulder high, steady and regular. Hawkers pass by selling Brazilian flags and curly green and yellow wigs. A group of pudgy, hungover Englishmen with farmer's tans are attempting to surf on bright green foam-top boards, drinking beer between two waves. A couple of them are passed out in the sand.

"So, why are you on Tinder?" Bruno asks, smiling slyly. He leans closer to you and you feel his eyes land on your bikini bottom. It is then that you notice the five crushed beer cans under his seat.

You draw your knees together and mumble something about making new friends, then slide your sunglasses on and close your eyes, digging your toes deep into the sun-warmed sand. As a child you spent days running on this beach. Your father used to tell you it was good for women to run in the sand, especially if they wore high heels often. Running in sand helps stretch the Achilles heel, he'd say.

"Eva? I'm talking to you."

You spot a black glint of anger in his eyes. You message Diego and ask him to call you, then pretext an emergency. You apologise profusely to Bruno, saying it was wonderful to finally meet him.

Back in an Uber, your shoulders slump in relief. You watch the day fade over the corrugated iron roofs of the sprawling favela.

Your phone lights up impatiently.

You're hot :)

You don't answer.

Then, twenty minutes later: Did you get my message?

And finally: I think the least you could do is reply.

You shut your phone off.

The next day, you go to two knockout matches and spend some time doing small talk with the officials. Diego picks you up after to go to a roda de samba. He takes one look at your black pants and leather flats and grins mischievously. You take the hint and grudgingly get changed. To you, Cariocas all look like they've just rolled out of bed.

As you push through the throngs around his friends' jam session, you are thankful you've downgraded to denim and have left your silver earrings at home. Diego brings you iced beer from a roadside stall with a Styrofoam cooler, kisses your forehead, and whispers in your ear how linda you are. He pulls you close and you dance body to body. You appreciate this show of ownership. When you are alone in Rio, even during the daytime, you feel painfully exposed by your whiteness.

That's what freedom is. Living without being watched.

At a street party farther down the road, electronic music is pulsing and men are kissing men. Modern people, Diego calls them. By now you have some level of trust in this garoto, but you are also acutely aware of the fact that it is 3am and you are in an unknown neighbourhood in a city known for its violence, entirely dependent on the goodwill of a guy you met on Tinder three days earlier and who clearly has a drug problem.

You attempt to look relaxed and fun-loving while discreetly committing landmarks and street names to memory. You try out your Brazilian slang with Diego's potbellied samba singer friend. He seems to find nothing abnormal about your presence in this group. Clearly, you are one of Diego's multitude of moças.

By 5am your feet are hurting and your head is beginning to pound. Diego waves down a taxi and promises to come join you in a couple of hours.

Your phone lights up just as you climb into the car.

Let's fuck. Where are you

You stiffen. You block Bruno on WhatsApp and remove him from Tinder. You message Diego to please come soon. The message gets delivered to his phone and you stare at it, anxiously waiting for the status to change to read.

You discreetly try to catch sight of the driver's GPS to track the journey. Your mind fills with stories of taxi drivers mugging their passengers at night, stripping them and dumping them on abandoned roadsides.

You see the name of your neighbourhood appear in blue letters on the screen. The tension in your shoulders evaporates. You survey the street, silent and restful in this end of the night. You have the driver stop 50 meters from your door so he doesn't know exactly where you live. But just as the taxi pulls away, your phone lights up with an SMS.

I know where you live.

In front of you, in the thick charcoal light, you see gnarled mango trees silently lining the street. A hand coming for you. Long carefree skips, heading down to the wide open sea.

There is so much freedom in being male.

Untitled
Lisha Zhong

Kwan-Ann Tan

Muar, 1941

for both my grandmothers.

We live in a house on stilts above the water, and at dawn
we shake off starlight, diving into the murky depths
of a mining lake. Like silver fishes, we play in water
that tastes of rust, marvelling at the way our skin
glitters in the sun. When tired, we lie on the dirt inert,
limbs a tangle of drowsiness. In this golden light our eyes
are as cloudy as the sickle-slit sap from a rubber tree,
the days passing like soap bubbles popping in the heat.

When the monsoon sweeps down from the mountains,
the lake overflows—lost treasures discovered, forgotten
toys. Empty shells, a spinning top, the final pieces
of a Chinese chess set, board splintered into fragments.
Carelessly skipping stones amidst the aftermath,
displacement haunted by sinking ships to the peninsula.
Innocence at this age is an opaque plume of smoke,
difficult to walk through, but dissipating in a blink.

And like lightning strike, the war: we follow the storm
back into hiding. My father wakes me in the dead of night,
the only witness to the funeral of a casket filled with gold.
In the day, my sister shears her hair short, dresses in
our older brother's castoffs. Our youngest sibling kept
quiet with a rag dipped in milk. Moving silently through
the sugar plantations, insects rising in a swarm at our
approach, the haze of sugar-cane holding us captive.

We blend into the forest, become the background to
a struggle we have no part in, the voiceless in any
great adventure. The sound of gunfire synonymous with
a rolling tropical tempest, stream running red with blood
no one can trace. Undaunted, we live between the leaves,
play the same games with a new companion, who
does not speak or sing. The tropical climate first
rots his flesh before his clothes, face peeled raw.

Jess Brown
You in Green

At the pond in August, near Keats' house
I added to its drops of green
And blurred up your body
Living again in the water

Your nutbrown form wore blue
And streamed out into
A duvet, your fingers
Curled on a page of Larkin;
We folded you into upturned turf.

Saline film makes rain of these scenes,
Collecting to fall,
Star light, to the ground

But where they sink you're found
Asserting that the leaves still grow
Above the lake, where buds have been
And you make light of all our black: in green.

Emily Robb
Blue

Here is a shell for you
Inside you'll hear a sigh
A foggy lullaby
  Joni Mitchell

When I draw now, bodies are blue.
Not rich or proud like Matisse,
but quiet, like no blood and no sleep.

Inside where I used to burn, this film
of blue tightens and sets:
fingers on a throat.

I have tried to lessen it, to warm myself
by the light of another but no sound could
be colder than the dim hiss of their candle
as it fizzles meekly out.

My blue always wins

Reuben Andrews
Face, Divine

"It is I. . .

                    . . .God!
Joseph peered deeper into his workshop.
He could not see me.
"Oh yeah?"
    "Yeah!" I replied, as thunderous as pans clanging against the base of
the ocean.
He thought for a moment, searching:
"Well if you're God, why don't you like do something
    . . .or whatever."
And so I p
        i
    s
        s
            e
            d o n t h e f l o o r.
Foam floated his sandals like rafts adrift at sea.
I smirked between the shadows.
        "Behold my child: gold."
"Gross! Not cool man!"
He approached my direction, the stench of urine betraying all.
    "Stop child! Do you wish to incur the grapes. . ."
"Is it wine you want?"
    ". . .of wrath?"
"Are you drunk?"
    "Ye dare, Joseph! The bloody cheek of you."
Grasping darkness, he brushed my ear and I scampered lowly as tax-
man on the prowl.

"I'm tired, whoever you are get out of my—"
But suddenly as he spoke, true lightning did:

S
  T
R
  I
K
  E

A bronchial cough rolled across the clouds,
    a spattered phlegm of hail rapped the roofing.

...back.   Joseph jumped...
To his knees,
 he grovelled.
   I laughed:
    "Do you see boy? Do you see now? Do you see clearly?"
"Y-yes my lord, please my L-Lord, please."
 With a hooded cloak about me I entered the light. Joseph winced at
these tattered rags.
   "This is my weekend form, Joe. Judge not."
"Y-yes; w-what do you want?"
 Long and hard did I   but eventually I reached a conclu-
sion. And let it be known that I said:
   "Give me pudding."
"W-we've got some at home my lord, can you fly us there?"
 "It is a nice night. Let's walk."

* ** *** **** ***** ****** ****

As we took to a sloping hill, Joseph frowned against the evening dust.
    I asked him: "What is it that cuts at you,
   son?"
He replied,

"I'm happy to see you my Lord, honest, but it's my girl. You see she's sweet as berries from the most berriful earth, and, uh, all that. But we argue non-stop. She says I work too much and too hard. My hands, full of splinters, can't hold her as she desires. My tired body can't produce the form she desires. Sawdust clings to my bones like wooden fleas on a. . . clockwork dog. We cry ourselves to sleep most nights. We're growing apart. What do you suggest Father?"

   "Oh. . .

           uh. . .

                      well Joe, you see, I. . .

                      have you tried. . .

                counselling?"

"Not yet, my Lord."

      "Well, do that, pal."

"Thanks God.   Can I call you God?"

      "Yeah, of course Joe."

He beamed for the first time in perhaps his entire life.

"Well, here we are."

      We entered into a modest shack –— Joseph paced towards his kitchen.

         Searching shelves and sighing, he returned to his melancholy:

"We're out of rice pudding.

I'll go shop, 10 minutes maximum.

Is Ambrosia okay?"

      "A tad sacrilegious, but I will allow it."

"Thanks God.

My girl is napping upstairs,

please try not to wake her."

And he left me

alone.

So I rifled his possessions; dropped pots and pans; purloined beads from
drawers; stroked his Labrador; waxed his—
  "Who are you?"

A voice like a scythe, behind me.
I almost snapped my neck to turn. . .
my god she was gorgeous, even shrouded in shadows.
  "I-I'm the Lord."
Half a glint shone from her teeth:
  "Oh yeah?"

Loneliness
Sara Pocher

E.M. Croft
Blue

When I was little, my best friend was called Suk Ya but her Australian name was Gracie. She was Korean. That doesn't mean she's not Korean now, she still is I guess, or maybe she never was. Her parents adopted her when she was just a baby and they made her an Australian, like me, and she got a toy koala and a green and gold certificate. I didn't have a certificate or a koala but Mum said she only had those things because she wasn't a real Australian. I dunno. There was something special about that piece of paper. It was official looking. Nice thick paper. Gold letters and everything.

The reason I don't know about Gracie now is because when we were ten Mum said we weren't allowed to play anymore and then she moved away. Mum said her parents overreacted to something that happened when her parents came to dinner and my uncle and aunt also came to dinner and my uncle complained about the slanty-eyed bastards who he did a job for in Sydney. Then Mr Frost, our teacher at school, made Gracie cry by yelling at her when we were drawing our self-portraits and she coloured her eyes in all black. Mum said that Gracie's parents overreacted again but we got a really nice new teacher called Miss French so my parents didn't complain to the school. But even though we got a new teacher, Gracie's parents sent her to a boarding school in the city and I never saw her again.

It's weird but I didn't have a best friend after that, even when I went to high school. The other kids treated me different and there were no other Korean kids in the town to make friends with, just the Chinese kids from the Chinese restaurant and they were older than me. I did date that guy in my last year of high school but I broke up with him because he told me that his mum was a Spanish model but my mum said that she was just a Filipino mail order bride. I didn't mind that she was

86

Filipino but I didn't want to go out with a liar. Plus, he told me he loved me after only four days of going out which I just didn't think could be right. Either you know right away or it grows on you. Four days just seemed off.

I hadn't thought about Gracie in years until I started going out with Abhi and my mum said it was just like me and that stuck up slopehead kid all over again. When I told her we were engaged, my mum called my aunt and she came over right away because she had seen this woman on A Current Affair who was the mum of a terrorist and she said she was proud of her son and would have more sons so they could also become terrorists. The Islamics have only one goal, my aunt said, and that was to breed terrorists. Mum said I didn't know what I was getting myself in for. Once I married him, she said, I wouldn't be protected by Australian laws anymore and would be punished under Sharia law where the men can do anything. I dunno. I wasn't really convinced because Abhi was always sweet, talking about how beautiful our wedding would be and how beautiful I would look in a sari. And his mum seemed really happy with his dad and she made amazing food. They also lived in this big house that they were going to give us once we got married because Abhi was their only child and they were downsizing to the Gold Coast. Talk about generous. We got everything. Like, everything. Right down to the weird blue statue with the four arms that I could never stop looking at even though it gave me the creeps.

But my aunt said she'd heard the same thing about Sharia law and if I think about it, maybe I did know something was wrong. I would be lying if I said that I didn't get a bit worried when my mum mentioned that Abhi could marry as many women as he liked. And, she said, if I even so much as looked at anyone else, he was allowed to honour kill me. So, yeah, I was a bit worried. But they say everyone gets cold feet.

My family still all came to our wedding, though. Abhi's parents paid for the wedding but my family brought their own booze. They didn't think to bring their own meat and my uncle kept asking Abhi's dad where the shish kebabs were. Abhi's dad was so confused and my uncle thought he couldn't speak English so kept asking the same question over and over, louder and louder. Then my aunt chipped in and there was a huge kerfuffle. Abhi eventually came over to explain to my uncle that there was no meat because they were hindi or something. My uncle stormed off and Abhi got real mad but in like a boiling-below-the-surface kind of way and when he asked me to stay away from my aunt and uncle I agreed just because I wasn't sure what he'd do if I didn't. I wouldn't exactly say I was scared of him but there was definitely something off. My uncle and aunt were loudly agreeing with each other that not eating meat was suspect. I was going to find all his other wives in a closet and come home crying, they said.

They were right. Basically. Abhi's parents gave us their house which was great at first because it's a really nice big house with six bedrooms and central air con and a pool. Abhi went to work every day but I didn't mind because I liked being at home alone with all the stuff. I used to make up little stories about where the items might have come from. The basket was handwoven by an old lady in a village who said that if you left it outside your front door on a full moon it would fill with dates but if you left it outside the door of your enemy it would fill with snakes. The mirror was given to her by a snake charmer who was in love with her but knew he couldn't marry her because he was poor so he gave her one of a pair of magic mirrors so that he could look at her whenever she looked in it. The little blue man with the four arms was a wedding gift from a guru that was a warning to her that husbands can have two men inside them and now this warning had been passed on to me.

I don't know what changed. Maybe nothing. Maybe everything. I do remember noticing that Abhi started to lose his tan. His parents came to visit and his mum got up me for not feeding him properly. You know when people feel sick and they turn a bit green? Well, because of his skin colour Abhi started to look blue. It was a bit gross, really. And every day I kept going around the house, dusting and rearranging, searching for something that I could never find. Finally, I just got sick of dusting all their useless crap.

I started going over to my aunt's place during the day because my mum was at work. We had to keep it a secret because I had technically promised Abhi that I wouldn't talk to her anymore. I don't know what gave it away in the end but somehow he knew and we had a huge fight.

At first I said that I didn't bloody care about going to my aunt's. I wasn't a loser. I had other things to do. If he wanted to forbid me from my aunt's like it was the secret bloody chamber then fine. But when he just accepted that I got really angry. Who was he to tell me what I could and couldn't do? I said that I didn't see what the big deal was but he said that was the problem. And the way he said it. Like he was cleverer than me or something. It was just so bloody condescending. So I told him that if he was so bloody clever he shouldn't have married me and that I only married him because I thought that he was different but I was clearly mistaken. And I said my family were right all along. Foreigners like him just didn't understand the Australian way of life. He couldn't control me. I was a free and independent woman. Why did he even marry me? I was certainly not going to be his free bloody ticket. Then I said that if he wanted to apologise he could find me in the bloody bath and I stormed off.

But he didn't come to find me. So I moved back home and a few months back Abhi asked for a divorce because he wants to get married again. I wonder if she's Australian, like me. You know, proper Australian. Maybe he has a taste for it now. Good luck to the stupid bitch, driving herself crazy, opening their cupboards, looking for parts of me.

Madeleine Pulman-Jones
Salt Water Foot Soak

I interrupt the smell of seawater when I walk
into the kitchen. The old lady is Greek.
Words slip from me like the tide.

She will wrap her feet in torn off strips of bedsheet.
Heating coffee, she throws her hands into meanings
I don't understand, like the saltiness that breathes

Its way to me from its hot bowl under the table.
We sit with it in a silence crowded with unfinish,
as she grammatically soaks each line of cotton,

before swaddling her feet, waiting for them to be
born again in this mustiness of salt-and-coffee-steam.
But not knowing pulls at my edges and I unravel –

I'm a sea of threads waving at the world in this
small and holy kitchen, like a channel-swimmer
just past exhaustion, the point of no return.

Salt seeps into the open weave. Wincing I get up to leave
worming an apology with new-born limbs,
and her eyes, shattering into crystals of reflective

blueness, say goodbye.

Niyousha Bastani
what are we when it rains

you speak warmer
than concrete, soft ambivalent
afternoon sky weeping, you say:
this is pathetic fallacy. grieving, i lie
pathetically: only a small rain.
you and i childish on this roof
we chase your laughs, we skip
the scene: one almost cold April
night almost clear your hands
pacing avoiding your heart
it does not want mine – the rain stops where
are we here when my body begs
let's go
and your frown tells me
let go
and the city shrinks
a map of our descent:
twisting stairs you say: it's easier to fight
going down. i imagine us
throwing axes to guard the heart i left
on the chapel roof, wet and hot, uncertain skies
the discomfort of no decisions made i like
not knowing for certain if
you scratch my hair curling silver already – don't
leave me (i can't read clocks
without you, time drips).
i don't scare you (much) so we drink
our iced coke on damp chairs it's August

yes, the heatwave seemed endless
before it ended, no fanfare fair warning
feet slip on roofs in rain
but let us ascend.
you bring a black umbrella
i laugh too much
too loudly for a girl
refusing dead things their ends, their rest.

Romana Pilepich
Exiting the Theatre

Having lived through the same play seen at
    different angles, the audience
    murmurs and splits into a
    crowd of individuals
    exiting the theatre
    and walking away at
        different angles. For a moment, the
          human stream wells up, coagulating at the edge of the overhang,
and then the first person
    steps into the night,
            pulling a string
                of similar others
                        out of the shelter
                        of the theatre's
                        yellow stone. The weak afternoon sun has long since set;
                        the stars' natural light is dim, obscured by
                        glowing streetlamps. The air gleams
with suspended droplets of water,
a lingering evening mist come
to cleanse them (symbolically)
without committing to the
theatrics of a thunderstorm.
          Some open umbrellas.
                                The night is quiet and empty.
                        Lighted postage-stamp windows
                  wink out into darkness, and the
              way home is as easy as the whisper
        of the curtain grazing the stage.

EXITING THE THEATRE

Only the occasional blue tram –
     whirring by smoothly on its tracks –

                                        punctuates

                                        the stillness.

Tom Bailey
Catching the Sun

So-and-so has caught the sun, you'd say,
and I'd wonder how they'd done it
and if I could do it too. Mammoth task:
starting with ledges and footholds,
clawing into flagstone and redbrick walls
and then swinging between balconies,
footsteps skipping over the tiles of rooftops,
climbing the ladders of endless skyline,
thirsty for a taste of the midday sun, hot jelly.
Now, at the top of a crane or the tallest tree
in sight, a hand reaching out in silhouette,
fingertips craving some thickness of cloud,
the hidden rafters of the sky to take me
even higher. And the people in the streets
below, gawping to see such fragile swaggering,
a child's figure teetering in the heavens.
Wings would make this easier, a more
effective, greedier Icarus, not just close
but touching, finally, when the evening comes
and the sun falls within reach, this fiery
little ball, cupped in the palms of my hands
and dripping with long licks of flame.
So-and-so has caught the sun, you'd say.

Tanvi Roberts
Echo

every word i said, girls, he'd hear his own voice
bouncing back at him – eureka!! an apple
on his head! like he'd invented gravity,
unfurled the double-helixed coils
of individuality. i'd speak &
he'd translate, my tremulous tones
would modulate into the deep BBC drone
of news, weather, bus announcements. at night
i'd practise conversations in the mirror
where everyone could hear my thoughts
unaccented, my legitimate frustrations
unwrought by the mysterious, ghostly wanderings
of some lonely womb. those conversations
the golden-spun threads of a loom, a story
where they would hear what wasn't said,
would stay to listen, not roll to the far side
of the bed, ask the questions i wanted
to answer, instead of teaching me silence.
unbelievable! it never grows old —
how a man steals your voice & calls you Echo.

Sarah Brady
I Climbed the Castle Mound, or Disillusionment

Last summer, around the time I was sitting my first university exams, a girl who I had met during fresher's week posted a picture on Facebook. It was her, and two friends, on top of the Castle Mound, captioned: "Finally made it xxx". If you are not a connoisseur of marginally-famous mounds, then please, allow me to enlighten you: The Castle Mound is just that. A mound that used to have a castle on it. It can occasionally be spotted towards the bottom of Cambridge University bucket-lists, such as "Thirty Things You Need to Do Before You Die (read: graduate)". I had never been.

The idea of standing on some Mound in the early morning wasn't a particularly attractive one, but I would've taken it over staring at a textbook for several hours.

A few weeks ago, I found myself in a similar position: half five in the morning, hunched over a desk, having experimentally eaten three teaspoons of instant coffee granules because I thought it would be more efficient than making a cup of coffee. My hypothesis was accurate, as per. I had not slept in thirty hours.

For whatever reason, my fifth essay in as many weeks could not hold my attention, so I checked Facebook; a friend of mine from school was active. I checked the time. Still five thirty.

"Why r you up at 5am for"

"Ayh sre u up for!!"

She had stayed in Newcastle for university and seemed to be having a good time – if the professionally-taken club photos were anything to go by. I hadn't been out in a long time. I hadn't done anything in a long time.

Slightly worried that my friend was drinking on a Thursday, I looked at the date and saw it was Sunday morning. Oh.

97

Quickly, I drew back from my desk. What kind of a student misses Saturday night? The kind sitting at their desk at half-past five on a Sunday morning, I supposed.

I spun on my chair for five minutes.

A bottle of gin decorated my shelf; it was useful as a book-stop.

I drank four glasses in an hour. All of a sudden, my time was finite, my youth was slipping through my fingers and I was going to die alone. My inebriated brain could only supply one solution: The Mound. I had to climb it. If not now, when? Soon I would be decrepit (twenty-one) and I would wish that I had climbed it while I had the chance. It had to be then and there.

I fell into the shower. About a minute in, I realised I was still wearing pyjamas. I had forgotten that I did not own a hairdryer. My hair was wet. It was February. That didn't matter. It was almost twenty-to-seven. I had to go.

I scavenged my bedroom floor for clean clothes – scratch that, any clothes — and I found a hip -flask instead. People drink to keep warm, right? I thought I had seen that before. People drinking to keep warm.

I filled the hip flask to the brim and got dressed. My hair was dripping down my neck and I needed to go.

I left.

Then I was at Queen's Green, retching against a lamppost. As I looked up, I could see the sky was turning. I was going to miss it. The dawn.

The further I walked, the more aware I was of the sting of my cheeks and the stiffness in my fingers. I could see my breath and feel my cold, wet hair sticking to my face. My hand pawed at my flask.

I would have used my phone to look for directions but the joints in my fingers were seizing up. So instead I followed a series of street signs which seem to point out of the city. Eventually, I found it. The Mound.

I felt cheated. I had half expected to see some medieval ruins. Some old stone bricks. Something. Anything that would've proven that a Castle had ever even been there. But there was nothing. There was only a commemorative plaque.

My attention drifted to the concrete steps which snaked around the side of the Mound. It was hardly a steep climb. I had climbed more intimidating hills to catch my morning bus when I was younger. The trick to going up hills, I told myself, was momentum. I wasn't sure how much of that I had left – given the gin.

I started off in a sprint but tripped on the first step. I had forgotten about falling over until a few days later when large purple bruises blossomed on my legs. I jogged the rest of the way up.

My pace slowed as I approached the top – not least because I could feel the phantom grip of childhood asthma squeeze tentatively at my lungs. Sat on the summit were two young women, shoulder-to-shoulder, wrapped up together in a tartan scarf. I was surprised. What kind of freaks were up this early on a Sunday? Suddenly, I was filled with dread. Oh God, what if they were Christians?

I concluded they probably weren't Christians when I saw the blunt.

The two women were in a world of their own, giggling and whispering in one another's ear. I overheard their game: one would try to make the other laugh by making up a ridiculous simile to describe how beautiful she was. "You're as beautiful as that tree. That one there." My hand gripped the hip flask.

They hadn't noticed I was there so I dragged my shoe against the rubble. Nothing. I scuffed my heel on the edge of the concrete step. One of the women leant in towards the other, tilting her head.

"Morning!"

Startled, she flung herself around to find the source of the outburst. I hadn't meant to shout it. Her shoulders slumped when she saw it was just a student and she turned back to her friend who had not-so-subtly shoved the still-burning blunt into her coat. They continued their word game, oblivious of me.

That was invitation enough for me to sit down.

I had overestimated the entertainment-value of the Mound by arriving twenty minutes early to see the dawn. Pulling my hood over the side of my face, I took a sip from the flask.

After sitting for a while, alone with my thoughts, I decided I needed a photo. I had walked all the way over. I needed a photo. It could be my cover photo on Facebook or something. "Finally made it xxx". I wanted a plaque – something I could show people.

My arm stretched out in front of me, I tried to take a selfie but they were all blurred. I was shivering too much. I couldn't keep still. I held my phone close to my face to inspect them. It didn't help; I was drunk. The pictures couldn't seem to capture what I wanted them to. I put my phone away.

Cambridge sprawled out before me; the silhouettes of medieval spires twisting against the foil of a morning sky which bled copper into pale blue. My eyes wandered from the University Library to King's Chapel, to St. John's, studying them. The city was still. As if it always had been. As if it always would be. I took another sip.

The women were getting more affectionate. I stood quickly and headed towards the steps. Before I left, I glanced back at the city.

"Bye," I said.

One of the women laughed.

I staggered back home through streets I had never before seen empty. The only other person I saw was when I peered over the edge of Magdalene Bridge at my reflection, rippling outwards on the surface of the water. I wanted to jump in. It would wake me up, I thought. I couldn't move, though. My hands were red-raw; fingers frozen to the railing.

I prised myself free and moved on.

The gin had made it difficult to coordinate my thoughts. I supposed that was the point. I had enough mental capacity to complete one action at a time. I focused on placing one foot directly in front of the other. One. Two. I walked the tight-rope down the middle of the road.

The sight of my building was a relief. My shivering had begun to feel like convulsions and my lips had cracked and were bleeding. My hair was damp.

I approached the electric doors. I looked up, briefly catching my reflection in the glass but the doors quickly slid open. The porter gave me a knowing smile. In fairness, he wasn't completely off the mark. It at least felt like a Walk of Shame.

     "Up a little early, aren't we?"

     "I've been on a walk."

     "Where to?"

     "The Castle Mound."

     "Never heard of it."

     "Oh."

Untitled
Lisha Zhong

Lizzi Hawkins
Elm

Not the branches, but the way the evening's
bottle-blue light falls through the branches,
not the trees, but the emptiness self-selecting
amongst trees. Any good observer will tell you
that spaces between are the real ingredient
of the thing — See: speech. See: molecules —
that love affairs exist best between acts two
and three, when we can imagine them
doing anything — frying pancakes, learning ju jitsu,
divvying up the school run — all the while their faces
giddy and radiant with love like two clean plates.
For we know that blame has to exist somewhere,
that we are all closet agoraphobes, needing
constriction to make sense of anything,
like politeness, or ribcages. And without this
how will you hold things, where will you sit
to square yourself against the terrible heft of the world?

Stranding

It was almost dark as Maggie walked back to the croft. She didn't believe in ghosts, but she started running uphill towards the house, thinking suddenly of the man's foot Matthew had found in a codfish after a week of gales. When he'd filleted it, his knife had hit a bone not pliant enough to be a fish's. Her grandmother said drowned souls were stuck in the sea, too shocked to leave the water. They wanted to pull the living towards them for company. They enticed people away from home, like the trowies who lured travellers into the hollow hills and made them play fiddle all night long. They poured the fiddlers glass after glass of wine, until the fiddlers stumbled, drunk, into daylight and realized a hundred years had passed.

Maggie knew those stories weren't true because she had never met anyone looking for people long dead. If trowies were real, you would — from time to time — meet someone in old-fashioned clothes, walking along the road, looking for people you'd never met.

She came to the gate at the top of the road and looked down to the beach. At first, a long new shelf of rock seemed to have risen up on the shore. A huge wave broke against it and a gleaming tail writhed forward then crashed down against the sand.

Then she realised it was dead, moving only in the waves.

The water swirled white around it. What she thought was rock resolved into a head, its snout blunt, flat, and tall as a shed door. Gashes ploughed down the body.

She thought of Matthew following those huge, slapping tails.

She had seen orca fins rise off the coast like black teeth. But she had never seen a whale like this, a whale as big as this, a whale that was anything but a speeding fin.

She thought of the scrimshawed whale teeth lying above the

hearth, teeth long as her forearm, covered in black crosshatched ships.

She turned around and walked back towards the small cluster of houses by the dock; Matthew, her husband, was gone for six months in the Antarctic, and someone should know about the whale.

The next morning, she walked down to the beach. Jack, her brother, stood beside the whale; its head was as tall as he was. He shouted to her. It was February now and they were almost out of meat; they'd been eating potatoes and the tough island kale that stayed green all winter. The men would start flensing the whale as soon as the tide went out, and there would be whale meat until spring. It tastes like beef, Jack said, except softer and milder, and a hint of fish.

That afternoon, she walked towards the beach again. The grass, lashed flat all winter by salt winds, was wet and pale against her boots, and the ground was soft in the new thaw.

She climbed up to the cliffs and lay on her stomach looking down. Bonxies dove and veered beneath her. The wind, full of the humid smell of blood, whipped her hair back.

She forced herself to watch. The blood on the beach did not frighten her if she did not think of it as blood. If she forced images to remain unconnected to thoughts, then red was a colour. A deep swathe of colour, darker at the centre, stamped with rings of a white froth like the white caps on waves. She had not seen anything this bright all winter.

Huge slabs of meat chequered the beach already like red flagstones. Where the flesh was sliced away, square indentations stamped the whale like recessed windows.

Two men cut a line in a new section of the whale – Jack and Peter lay on their stomachs on top of the whale. The other men worked from the beach. Together they peeled back a new section of the spik; it came away like a huge sheet, and it fell on the ground, gelatinous and pale as puss.

All the men were covered in blood now. She thought of her husband; in the Antarctic, on Matthew's ship, men wore spikes on their shoes to keep from slipping in the whale blood. Matthew's spiked boots sat in the loft all summer. He was wearing them now, and icebergs loomed around him taller than their house.

A coiled, enormous white mass rose up out of the blood. Slowly Maggie realized what it was: the whale's intestines bulged from its side.

She made herself keep watching. The guts looked muscular, a mass that could lash free with its own jiggling, coiled strength.

Finally they sagged forward, and men wrestled them clear of the whale's stomach. Maggie felt sick. She kept watching. Observation renders experience down to a handful of images and sensations. On their own, those mean nothing. They can only appal when you let them all snap together like magnets.

When the men finally went home, Maggie kept lying on the cliff. Slowly, she got up and climbed down the grassy hill towards the bay.

She had never smelled blood like this: she had seen sheep slaughtered, but this was different. She walked to the whale's head and crouched beside its gaping mouth, which was full of the humid scent of rotten fish. She wanted to run, but she had thought all day about this whale.

She could not shake the feeling that some trickster god was perched nearby, cutting her a deal: if she reached out and touched this whale, Matthew would arrive home safely. Somewhere, weaving between icebergs, his ship balanced between danger and security. If she overcame her revulsion, a capricious spirit would keep her husband safe. That was a superstitious thing to think; she knew that. But what if her thinking it was mad allowed a flinty god to win after she had walked away from a game she didn't believe existed?

The blood had seeped into the sand where she walked along the mouth, which was as long as their sheep shed. White teeth splayed out sharply like the bleached ribs of a wrecked ship.

Without the blood and the smell, the whale wouldn't have seemed like an animal. It was huge – geologic, more like cliffs and sea stacks than like any animal she'd ever known.

Its bottom jaw was stuck hanging down, wide open. The rest of the head swelled up huge behind it, its eye level with Maggie's head. The mouth smelled like rotten fish, humid and close. The closed eye domed up, tiny in the mass of the whale's head. Its heavy tongue swelled, bluish gray, between the teeth.

She breathed in the wind off the sea, turning away from the rotten scent rising from that raw throat, and wrapped her hand around one tooth. The corrugated enamel dug into her palm, but her littlest finger was brushing the gum, which was cold and so clammy she thought her hand would stick to it.

She raced up the beach, then stopped. The reflex to run, she realized, had outlasted fear, which had subsided into something methodical and quiet. She walked back to the whale. She could hear the waves sucking sand away from the whale as they crashed up and then contracted back into the sea. She put her hand flat beneath the whale's eye. Its skin was cold and smooth as metal. Under her hand, the whale was quiet. The noise of men shouting was over. Finally, what remained of its body was still. She sat next to it until it got dark, and then stayed on. She didn't want to leave it alone, so newly dead. Half its body was gone and its ribs arced out like an upside down ship's frame. But the head was still there. The face was still intact, so large it lost the sense of being a face. She could still just see the whale's head rising above her, a denser, more defined patch of darkness. The wind picked up, carrying the cold in off the sea. She slipped her hands into opposite sleeves of her sheepskin jacket. Then she stood and put her hand against the whale again. This was the quiet that made people say that, just past what you can hear, the hills are full of fiddlers, and whoever hasn't come home might be lost, or might be in those hills, playing all night, wondering how to leave.

Meg Freeman
John Donne

She says the separation makes her seasick.
Instead, she keeps his shoes shipshape and sleeps besides the seafront
repeating No Man Is An Island. She paints with his freckles,
lives like an anchoress but goes to church in a morning
and walks through the ocean to the surface. She
remembers slipping her fingers through pebbles whilst kneeling —
thinking — 'This man is MY island.' Strands herself
beyond the tides, knows his body less like home and more
like a dying sailor swept ashore. She lays waiting as the water dissolves.
She's kept afloat by those goodbye thoughts and stories he tells

of what lies onboard, not rumours of women less explored. Sees the
lipstick on his shirt as a mark of men kissed by the sun and

keeps her suspicions bottled. She gets the call to tell her the news
that unlike the house they built, submerged
he'd died in the open of her arms, pressed into a needle point, on land,
by the car. Like light from afar, words they fractured and merged —
Plenty of fish in the sea. Plenty of fish in the sea.
Like sunlight from afar, his vows lay fractured like
salt shards as his body dies in her arms. She was driving in a car
to their house. That news meant that, like the house built for fishermen,
their love remained caught and bottled. Got the call to tell her. His corpse

was packed and pieced back together to come back home. A man defined
by truths of what lies ashore. Now, his drowned freckles grow from the
ground —
not the dying sailor washed up and wasted, but a body formed into

mountain. A man come home. She is kept afloat by sympathetic
moans like: that man was a beautiful island, you know? Stranded,
she now imagines running her fingers through the pebbles and keeps

thinking of his freckles bleeding into her lap. Goes to church in a morning
and lives like an anchoress on knees cut with shells.
Repeats and keeps his shoes shipshape and sleeps
beside the seafront, thinking: this separation keeps me sea-sick.

Gabriella Attems
Hortus Conclusus

The moon processes the high grasses
into shadow and silver; it weaves no
flute music, no dance. It gloats at my pale
hands, my empty errand at the black gate.
The alley lined with trees brings only the screech
of night-fowl, the bridge white and empty.
Didn't riders used to come, huntsmen, rangers,
falconers shouting Open! Let me in!
The moon has cancelled the stars.
What do you want? it asks, owl-bright
above the courtyard, the motherwort
and weeds. The chestnuts quiver,
furtive rivulets of light on their limbs,
their bark bathing in a touch of silver.

John Phipps
The End

He walks home drunk at night, convinced
he is right about everything. He walks past the wet ferns
that stand in the mist of their greenness, the opal-hung web
in its orionic glister, the cherry blossom lost
by the orange lamplight loosed through it. He walks home drunk,
ever-more convinced that he is right,
as years pass, muttering to themselves,
and the road grows longer and the night grows shorter.
He is always right about everything.
He leans forwards, you see, leans out over the edge
of a glorious understanding, a complete consummation
and this leaning out and over explains the downward weight
he feels. The sudden moments where he thinks
he's falling. Always too this troubling over love,
the having and the getting of it, its slow going away,
hearts in their summer-evenings fade,
Venus coming and going each night, then going away
for the last time, without saying, gathering her things
and quietly hitching the gate behind her at dawn,
and he wonders about it, as he walks home drunk
along the deepening groove of the year,
as his friends disappear suddenly, as the pooled decades
transpire like water from the dipped crown
of holly, the daffodils and snowdrops come and go
like power surges in unshaded bulbs,
faster and faster, the blossom fusing up and out,
a white-gold firework, and gone as soon,
the whole world heaving with shortened breath

as he walks home drunk and knows he's going nowhere,
looking through the black rumble of what waits
to where distance conceals itself in a long V,
straining to see beyond which vanished point
nothing will come together silently
with nothing, black petals opening about
the stars, and all their bright conviction spent.

Contributors

VIDA ADAMCZEWSKI is a third-year Philosophy, Politics, and Economics student at Wadham College, Oxford. She gets more like her mother every day.

REUBEN ANDREWS is a second-year Law student at Fitzwilliam College, Cambridge.

ANONYMOUS is interested in the concept of trying to establish an identity in the Age of Information and Over-sharing, as well as reflective materials.

GEORGIOS-SPYRIDON ATHANASOPOULOS is a trained architect and computational designer. His ongoing PhD research at the Department of Engineering, University of Cambridge focuses on the development of innovative geometric computational methods to facilitate collaboration between structural engineers and designers.

GABRIELLA ATTEMS is a second-year Creative Writing student at Kellogg College, Oxford. She likes to probe the idea of enclosure vs. that of freedom.

TOM BAILEY is a third-year English student at St John's College, Cambridge. His work has been published in Agenda's Online Broadsheet, The Kindling, The Blue Knib, and The Cambridge Student, among other places.

NIYOUSHA BASTANI is a first-year Politics and International Studies PhD student at St John's College, Cambridge. She worries about the politics of security and care.

SARAH BRADY is a second-year Modern and Medieval Languages student at Newnham College, Cambridge. She is incredibly passionate about the Franco-Prussian war of 1870. Needless to say, she is also great fun at parties.

JESS BROWN is a third-year English student at St Anne's College, Oxford. She helped to launch (and went on to edit) the Oxford Review of Books.

GRACE CRABTREE is a third-year Fine Art student at St Anne's College and the Ruskin School of Art, Oxford. She has just ordered a vast box of pigments, probably to paint with but definitely to enjoy gazing at all the colours.

DAN CRITCHLOW-WHITAKER is a second-year Chemistry PhD student at Clare College, Cambridge. His poetry is an often gritty reflection of the rural Yorkshire landscapes that raised him.

E.M. CROFT is an MSt student in Creative Writing at Lucy Cavendish College, Cambridge. She is interested in intergenerational relationships, the concept of 'the other' and probing the liminal space between mathematics and everything else.

THOMAS DAVIDSON is a fourth-year Computer Science student at Corpus

Christi College, Cambridge. His main inspirations are the interaction of light and dark as well as the combination of digital and analogue media.

ANNA DOBROWOLSKI is a Master's student of Comparative Literature at St Edmund's college. Her work is inspired by natural history and pathology in both art and literature.

VALK FISHER is a Creative Writing postgraduate (MSt candidate, 2020) at Selwyn College, Cambridge. Valk is an essayist, poet, critic and nonfiction writer whose work gravitates towards politics, culture, gender and the body, often exploring points of intersection.

MEG FREEMAN is a second-year English student at Newnham College, Cambridge. She enjoys writing about how domestic and natural spaces interact.

KATHARINA FRIEGE is a DPhil History student at St Hugh's College, Oxford. She works on notions of identity and belonging.

ESME GARLAKE is a fourth-year Modern Languages student at Robinson College, Cambridge. She loves filling up notebooks, writing songs on her guitar and recycling.

MARY GATENBY is a third-year Fine Art student at St Edmund Hall, Oxford. She is interested in Celtic folklore and methods for the creation of histories and traditions.

MATHIAS GJESDAL-HAMMER is a third-year HSPS student at Christ's College, Cambridge. He is especially interested in 20th century American photography from Walker Evans and Robert Frank to Jeff Wall.

CLOVER GODSAL is a third-year Arabic and Middle Eastern Studies student at St Catharine's College, Cambridge. She likes drawing and is currently based in Egypt.

ZÉBULON GORIELY is a second-year Computer Science student at Queens' College, Cambridge. In his digital art he likes to explore surreal elements, drawing influence from Magritte and Escher.

LIZZI HAWKINS is a final-year Engineering student at Corpus Christi College, Cambridge. Her debut pamphlet, Osteology, was published by Smith|Doorstop in 2018.

ANGUS JACKSON is a second-year English student at Jesus College, Cambridge. He has recently developed an interest in prison literature and his piece, 'birthday', was prompted by participation in 'Writing Together', a creative writing programme run between Cambridge University's 'Learning Together' and HMP Whitemoor.

MARIE-LOUISE JAMES is a third-year Modern and Medieval Languages student for German and Italian at Trinity College, Cambridge. She started learning sculptural drawing with classical training in Florence, Italy, where during hours in the studio she and her then 14-year-old big brother would tease each other and make mini-sculptures out of kneaded putty rubbers.

WALTER JONES is an MSt. Creative Writing student at Wolfson College, Cambridge.

RILEY KAMINER is an MPhil candidate in Latin American Studies at Sidney Sussex College, Cambridge. He is fascinated by the intersection of media and politics, particularly in the Spanish-speaking world.

JOANNA KAYE is a fourth-year English and Spanish student at Somerville College, Oxford. She finds that writing is a space where difficult, painful subject matters can be better understood.

ELLE LAVOIX is pursuing an MSt in Creative Writing at the Institute of Continuing Education, Cambridge. An advocate for women's and children's rights, her work focuses on structural power dynamics and vulnerabilities linked to the digital world.

JEROME LIM is a Singaporean postgraduate student reading Modern & Contemporary Literature at Gonville & Caius College, Cambridge. His poetry sequence 'Archipelago' was awarded the Ursula Wadey Memorial Prize in 2018.

KRYSTOFER R. MACKIE is a fourth-year Philosophy and French student at Pembroke College, Oxford. He is particularly interested in making nonsense.

CATHERINE MACNAUGHTON is a first-year English student at Wolfson College, Cambridge, where she is searching for inspiration.

ZOË MATT-WILLIAMS is a first-year English student at Downing College, Cambridge. Her interests include bright patterns, thinking about the intersection of art and politics, and Sainsbury's chocolate oranges.

JENNY O'SULLIVAN is a fourth-year Modern and Medieval Languages student at King's College, Cambridge. As a queer, dyslexic northerner, Jenny writes plays, draws comics and performs drag, united by an interest in illegibility.

NESEM PETEK OZBEY is a fourth-year PhD student in Molecular Biology at Murray Edwards College, Cambridge. She likes painting about dreamy situations.

RUARI PATERSON-ACHENBACH is a third-year Music student at Girton College, Cambridge. His work in graphic scoring is inspired by the multi-media compositions of Claudia Molitor and text pieces by Pauline Oliveros, and hopes to promote sonic creation deeply tied to themes of intimacy, nostalgia, and transience.

DIANA PAULDING is an MPhil student in Hebrew Bible at Fitzwilliam College, Cambridge. She studies trauma in the Old Testament and procrastinates by looking at manuscripts and learning dead languages.

LEVIN PFEUFER is an Arts, Creativity, and Education MPhil student at Fitzwilliam College, Cambridge. Levin works across a wide range of arts methods, both in his own practice and with youth charities.

JOHN PHIPPS is an MSt student in Early Modern Studies at New College, Oxford. He edits the Oxford Review of Books.

ROMANA PILEPICH is an MPhil student in Environmental Policy at Lucy Cavendish College, Cambridge. She is inspired by light.

SARA POCHER is a second-year Chinese student at Homerton College, Cambridge. She is an avid reader, a compulsive doodler and an incorrigible daydreamer.

MADELEINE PULMAN-JONES is a second-year Russian and Spanish student at Trinity Hall, Cambridge. She likes thinking about Soviet cinema, autobiographical fiction, and Georgian food.

GRACE RICHARDSON is a master's student at St Catharine's College, Cambridge. She is currently writing a thesis about truth and triviality, which sounds a bit like an undiscovered Jane Austen novel but is sadly nowhere near as interesting.

EMILY ROBB is a third-year English student at Emmanuel College, Cambridge. She runs a feminist magazine, Staunch, and hopes to pursue a career in writing after graduation.

TANVI ROBERTS is a second-year Classics student at Clare College, Cambridge. She likes thinking about different concepts of love in ancient Greek and Latin literature.

ALFIE ROBINSON is a second-year Art History student at Downing College, Cambridge. Materials are his main source of inspiration; he is particularly passionate about surface coatings.

KATHERINE ROBINSON is a PhD candidate in English at Pembroke College, Cambridge. Her fiction and poetry have appeared and are forthcoming in The London Magazine, The Kenyon Review, The Hudson Review, Poetry Wales, Poetry Ireland, and elsewhere.

ALISA SANTIKARN is a first-year Archaeology PhD student at Jesus College, Cambridge. She likes playing with paint.

MATTHEW SECCOMBE is a third-year Architecture student at Jesus College, Cambridge. He specialises in sketches and line drawings of which most are drawn on location.

EVAN SILVER is a master's student in English at King's College, Cambridge. He is a multidisciplinary writer, director, and composer.

DANIELLE SILVERMAN is a MPhil South Asian Archaeology student at St John's College, Cambridge. Her poetic inspiration comes from her travels overseas and from raising chickens.

KWAN-ANN TAN is a second-year English student at Jesus College, Oxford. She can often be found obsessively mapping out various tarot paths of her future or researching where to buy ambergris.

LUCY TILLER is a second-year English student at St Catharine's College, Cambridge. She likes nonsense poetry and campaigning for nuclear disarmament.

BEN VINCE is a second-year English student at Gonville & Caius College, Cambridge. His main area of interest is the confessional in poetry.

HOPE WHITEHEAD is a third-year English student at Queens' College, Cambridge. She has always loved literature but she also enjoys writing about film.

EVELYN WHORRALL-CAMPBELL is an MPhil student in Film and Screen Studies at Pembroke College, Cambridge. She is currently swimming in posthuman waters.

LISHA ZHONG is a second-year Natural Sciences student at Downing College, Cambridge. She likes the quieter side of things.

Sponsors

ALL SOULS COLLEGE, OXFORD
CHRIST'S COLLEGE, CAMBRIDGE
CHURCHILL COLLEGE, CAMBRIDGE
EMMANUEL COLLEGE, CAMBRIDGE
EXETER COLLEGE, OXFORD
GONVILLE AND CAIUS COLLEGE, CAMBRIDGE
HOMERTON COLLEGE, CAMBRIDGE
JESUS COLLEGE, CAMBRIDGE
JESUS COLLEGE, OXFORD
LUCY CAVENDISH COLLEGE, CAMBRIDGE
MAGDALENE COLLEGE, CAMBRIDGE
MERTON COLLEGE, OXFORD
NEW COLLEGE, OXFORD
NEWNHAM COLLEGE, CAMBRIDGE
PEMBROKE COLLEGE, CAMBRIDGE
QUEENS' COLLEGE, CAMBRIDGE
ROBINSON COLLEGE, CAMBRIDGE
ST EDMUND HALL, OXFORD
ST JOHN'S COLLEGE, OXFORD
THE QUEEN'S COLLEGE, OXFORD
TRINITY COLLEGE, CAMBRIDGE
WADHAM COLLEGE, OXFORD
WOLFSON COLLEGE, CAMBRIDGE